DISCOVER YOUR
POWER
Heal TO

Phyllis Ann Giarraffa MSN, PMH NP

i

ABOUT THE AUTHOR

Phyllis Giarraffa is presently licensed as a Psychiatric Nurse Practitioner who graduated with her Master's Degree from the University of North Carolina at Chapel Hill. She attended medical school at the University of Montserrat of Science, Art, and Technology. She completed her MSN and BSN at the Medical College of Georgia more than 30 years ago. For the last 30 years, she has been working in the psychiatric field and, more recently, the State Hospital in Savannah, Georgia.

During the past 10 years, she has been active in both inpatient and outpatient mental health counseling. She is a Sigma Theta Tau member, a nursing scholarship organization, and certified by the American Nurses Credentialing Center.

Phyllis has traveled extensively and lived in various places with her family, living in Curacao's Dutch Caribbean island for several years. They traveled to India, trekking the Great Himalayas to various spiritual Sikh holy sites. These include Gurudwara Sri Hemkunt Sahib, a Sikh place of worship and pilgrimage site in Chamoli district, Uttarakhand, India, and are the highest of the Sikhs, located at an altitude of 14,203 feet. It is a holy shrine that received its name from the glacial lake Hemkund (Lake of the Snow).

This temple is only accessible by foot for about ¾ mile walking a difficult path at track angles in some places 60-75 degrees with additional stairs of rock stones. Due to its elevation, some people can have difficulty breathing. This pilgrimage is of the Sikh's 10th teacher, Sri Gobind Singh, where he meditated and gained spiritual strength and insight. Additional traveling includes trips throughout Europe and twice to Italy, the place of her parent's origin.

INTRODUCTION

While I was preparing for my retirement this past year during the time of COVID-19, an interesting phenomenon occurred. A friend of mine had a torn rotator cuff, and due to COVID, her elective surgery had been canceled. Unable to bear the pain, she asked if I might be able to perform spiritual healing on her, just to hold her over until the surgery. To my surprise, after our session, my friend's shoulder had been completely healed. When it was time for her surgery, she decided to cancel it altogether.

How was this possible?

Had spiritual healing contributed to this physical healing? Months have passed since then, and she is still pain-free with no reoccurrence. Over the next few months, I worked with many other patients who have reported permanent healing, which was an exciting phenomenon.

My first influence entering the healing field was my father's encouragement, a chiropractor with a fascination for psychic powers. He gained his desire from watching Israeli Uri Geller bend utensils (mainly spoons) on TV. My father possessed a strong belief that healing was possible and that our hands are a powerful tool.

A practicing Catholic, my father believed strongly that Jesus was the most potent healer. He thought others could possibly do the same. When I was a teenager, he encouraged me to heal myself, prompting me to become a "self-healer" instead of taking pain medications. Even then, I remember feeling God's power and energy as I closed my eyes and focused on healing. As I grew, I became interested in yoga and meditation. At age 17, I taught yoga for a semester in my senior gym class at my Catholic High School.

After graduating, I began to attend college. However, to my parent's disappointment, I dropped out to live at the Kripalu yoga center. When I left the Kripalu yoga center in my twenties, I began searching for spiritual direction. It was at this point in my life I met Dolores Saunders. Dolores was teaching at Carnegie Hall and opened my mind to healing and medium-ship.

She introduced me to psychometry methods: the ability to discover facts about an event/person by touching inanimate objects associated with them or within their energy field. Dolores also instructed me in energetic and spiritual healing. Though I did not find psychometry to be an art I could be successful in, I discovered I was naturally gifted as a healer.

A few years later, I married my husband, my true soul mate, and an Indian, Sikh man. I learned various healing modalities such as Healing Touch and Reiki Healing and learning about Sikhism throughout the years.

While married in my 30s, I had a visit or apparition of Jesus, which altered the course of my life. As I slept, Jesus appeared to me. He descended down from the heavens, floating on a misted cloud, shrouded in a golden aura. Pure love poured from His eyes as He gazed upon me, and my soul filled with warmth, unlike that I had ever felt before. He reached out his hand to me and told me it was time, he had something to teach me, and I had to go with him, just for now.

Stunned by the pure awe of his presence, I could barely think, let alone speak. My first thought was that I wanted to share this experience with my soul mate. I responded by asking, "Can my husband come with us?" He said, "No, I am only a symbol for him." My husband is a Sikh, and most world religions recognize Jesus as an important religious figure. They do make efforts to account for His existence and teachings. Modern Jews even accept Jesus was a rabbi or popular teacher, and accept he had supernatural abilities to perform miracles, but not that He was the Messiah.

I believe that he embraces and loves all people from all religions, and I was honored that he had chosen to visit and teach me. He guided me from my room towards the heavens, and I watched as everything I knew faded away into the golden oneness of His grace. We entered an inner room with a large book, and I knew this was His book, the book of His actual teachings.

It was clear why it had taken nearly four decades of studying various spiritual practices before He showed me his teachings. There is a saying: the moment the student is ready, the teacher appears. In my case, it was the Master. Only when the student is prepared for knowledge can the knowledge be given. Throughout my life, this knowledge was passed over time, preparing the ground for sowing.

I had to grow, develop, and nourish to plant the harvest. We often try to devour truth but digest little so slowly over time. I could now learn to do as instructed. My consciousness needed to learn to apply the knowledge given.

When He left the room, he ascended back into the mist, floating gracefully; in the same manner, he first entered the room.

There were two similar occasions where He came to me in such a grand manner, to bless me and repeat His teachings.

During these blessings, I was prostrated at His feet. As I gripped the hem of His robe, I was content to spend eternity there before him. When I arose, He placed His hand to my forehead. The moment His finger brushed my skin, a series of lights of every color bled from Him into me. He has continued to visit me now at night, teaching me, though His messages are imparted to me more telepathically. Usually, I awake in the morning with the memory of His messages or of His image.

I really didn't know what to do with any of this at the time. Returning to my roots, I went back to the Catholic Church with this new worldly perspective, hoping to receive directions on what to do next. Now 30 years have passed, and I have been exposed to many other spiritual traditions. I was raised Catholic, so I will always consider that tradition my sacred home. I have embraced many more traditions, such as the Unity Church and Sikhism, which are open to receiving all in their congregations. These have provided me spiritual nourishment upon which I can draw for myself and those of my clients.

PREFACE

Spiritual healing and alternative healing practices are becoming more widely recognized by the general public of the West. Despite its many advances in health care, the medical industry has increased costs, fed addictions to opiates, and has, in many ways, increased people's expectation of treatment and symptom alleviation – with little or no focus on how to prevent the conditions of disease in the first place.

New or alternative approaches to healing have presented different options to people that are more cost-effective than Western medicine while still maintaining a high quality of health and care. Spiritual healing has been viewed through a skeptical lens by many in the medical field despite the consistently positive evidence and research that continues to be gathered.

For spiritual healing to gain sufficient interest and respect as a genuine option for disease prevention and treatment, I believe there needs to be additional objective, scientific research. And a review of the evidence supporting the phenomena has personally experienced it again with my clients.

Spiritual healing has not been given proper appreciation. As I share this book with you. My intention is to acknowledge the great benefits and power of spiritual healing by sharing my personal journey, testimonials of those I have healed, and research that supports these events. For the sake of my client's privacy, I have changed their names. Spiritual healing is not the end-all in all situations.

The healing process can often be even more effective when spiritual healing modalities are combined with allopathic healing techniques. This partnership can accelerate the healing process and promote harmony throughout the mind, body, and spirit.

This is one of many examples in which we, as a collective, must realize there is no one answers to a given problem. There is no wrong and right; instead, that is an illusion of division that we overcome. Spiritual healing and allopathic techniques are two sides of the same coin, and ignoring one for the other only furthers this false dichotomy.

The pages that follow are meant to be a tool and a resource for anyone who reads them. Even more specifically, this book has the power to be a life-changing and potentially life-saving tool for those of you who:

➢ Yearn to access your innate power to heal yourself!
➢ Have an open mind and an interest in alternative approaches to healing that can be practiced without undesirable side effects!
➢ Are you experiencing something deemed incurable by traditional medicine but have not given up hope and believe your symptoms, condition, illness, or disease is, indeed, curable!
➢ Want to learn how to be healthy while still healthy, not when it's already too late!
➢ I no longer want to be in pain, whether chronic or temporary and have a genuine desire to lead a healthy, balanced, empowered life!
➢ Are you willing to explore the question: "What else can I do for my illness, disease, or condition that will not put me

at risk financially, physically, emotionally, and/or spiritually?"

There is great value in accepting and practicing spiritual healing techniques. Throughout the book, I'll address different healing barriers, ways to identify those barriers, and practices that will help you overcome these barriers. I hope to show you the power of this healing mode as a primary or complementary practice in your healing journey.

Welcome to my journey

DEDICATION

This book is dedicated to my husband Jasbir Mokha who has recently been stricken with Alzheimer's. It has been emotionally challenging to be a caretaker, work full time, and carry on my healing work. My parents who raised me lovingly which was so important for spiritual development. My children Amar, Nick and his wife Gail. They all have been patient with me during my years studying spiritual and educational studies. My husband's extended family and all of my family.

Our local priest, Father Gabe, at St Frances Cabrini Catholic Church here in Savannah, Georgia who has supported my healing journey. My friend Darlene DeGumbia whom is the person that first had a spontaneous healing which was when I had the realization of the power of healing. My friends and colleagues where I am employed at Georgia Regional Hospital in Savannah. Hopefully, this book will create a spiritual awakening in each of you!

CONTENTS

about The Author iii

Introduction v

Preface ix

Dedication xii

Chapter 1 : Embracing Spiritual Healing 1

    Electrical Activity In The Human Body 3

    Approaches To Healing 4

    The Healing Session 5

    Energy Centers And Pathways 7

    Spiritual Healing As A Complementary Component To

    Conventional Medicine 9

Chapter 2 : Physical Barriers To Health 12

    Physical Reasons For Not Healing 16

    Preventive Measures 17

    Yogic Benefits 19

    Stem Cells - The Dawning Of A New Age Of Medicine 20

Chapter 3 : Spiritual Tools For Healing 22

Chapter 4 : The Power Of The Mind To Heal 38

    What Do We Mean By Manifestation? 39

    Our Story And Regulating Self-Talk 40

    Feel It Real 42

    Visualization 45

    Sound Healing 46

    Faith 48

Chapter 5 : Psychological Barriers To Health 50

Chapter 6 : Physical And Spiritual Balance 61

Yamas 62

Niyamas 63

Asana 63

Pranayama 63

Pratyahara...64

Dharana...64

Dhyana 64

Samadhi 65

Additional Yoga Information 65

Chapter 7 : Human Energy Centers 69

Chapter 8 : The Dark Night Of The Soul................................77

The Spiritual Process Of The Dark Night 78

Health..80

The Collective's Dark Night...81

Gratitude, The Answer To Worry 83

Chapter 9 : The Kingdom Of Heaven Is At Hand....................86

Chapter 10 : Integrative Healing For The Future....................95

Reflections 100

Meditation 102

Routine..104

CHAPTER 1
EMBRACING SPIRITUAL HEALING

What if I told you that there is a power within you right now that can initiate healing throughout your mind, body, and spirit?

It's true; self-healing power exists within you! This form of healing is called *spiritual healing*. Spiritual healing is not a newly discovered form of healing; it can be traced back to biblical times, and even before that. However, its popularity has grown significantly in recent years.

Spiritual healing is a process that takes place between a higher source of energy – which I regard as God – a practitioner, and a patient. As a spiritual healer, the practitioner is an alternative health care professional capable of assisting individuals in realizing their innate ability to heal themselves through the transfer of energy. The healing energy transferred from practitioner to patient promotes intense relaxation and the release of built-up physical, emotional, mental, and spiritual tension.

Together, the healer and the client set an intention to achieve optimal results of the healing session. The session can begin with both individuals speaking a prayer or affirmation to allow an open connection to the divine. This is called centering and allows both to enter a meditative state, or time of silent intention.

The intention of spiritual healing is to remove negative energy, to clear out a toxic internal environment, and make room for clean, positive, and healthy energy to exist. The patient and the practitioner can both expect to feel physical, emotional, and spiritual changes throughout the healing process.

After an intention is set, the spoken word is used minimally to allow the client to be sensitive to and feel the subtler forces at work. There is little physical touch during a healing session, instead the practitioner gently massages the *energetic*, not physical, body. It's important to be open to all possibilities and not have any specific expectations – healing may occur in a way that is unexpected, and may at points be emotionally uncomfortable as these patterns are being released but is happening nonetheless. I find it important to note here, that it is always important use one's power of *discernment* and *intuition* about their own level of comfort and personal safety with any kind of practitioner – homeopathic or allopathic.

A spiritual healer's responsibility is to provide a safe space for relaxation, visualization, and intentional healing; in doing this the healer actually assists a client in learning how to access the divine healing potential within each of us, and their own ability to heal themselves and others. Though the practitioner is the catalyst, the healing ultimately occurs through the client's release of these negative energies and emotional patterns, and their embrace of the healing by accepting all that can happen in the session.

It is often assumed that spiritual healing is associated with a religious affiliation when, in fact, its powers are universal. The outcome of spiritual healing is not dependent upon the patient's beliefs and values and entirely reliant on the patient's willingness to remove their own spiritual, psychological, and physiological barriers to healing. One must have a genuine desire to heal to experience the effects of spiritual healing.

ELECTRICAL ACTIVITY IN THE HUMAN BODY

To fully understand the process of spiritual healing and what is taking place during a healing session – regarding how the transfer of energy induces healing – it's essential to know how the human body functions in relation to the electrical activity taking place within the body.

There is a term called "bioelectricity." This refers to electrical 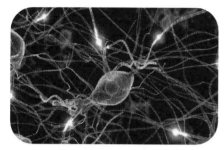 currents produced within the human body. These are generated by a variety of biological processes. Put simply, bioelectricity (pictured) is the term used to describe how the trillions of cells in the human body carry electrical potential and continuously communicate with each other.

Suppose a person can learn to tap into this bioelectric network, which controls the body. In that case, they can, to a certain degree, train the cells to assist in healing when an illness or disease manifests itself. Since the cells are in constant communication with one another, interrupting the cellular conversation is necessary to redirect the cells towards the area of the body that requires healing.

As a spiritual healer, my role is to channel healing energy from God to the trillions of cells in my patient, guiding the cells towards the illness, disease, pain, or trauma, thus improving the efficiency of the body's healing forces.

APPROACHES TO HEALING

There are various approaches to spiritual healing that ultimately promote harmony throughout the mind, body, and spirit without prescription medications, over-the-counter drugs, or any other conventional medical intervention. In all spiritual healing modalities, the healing that takes place is made possible through the transfer of universal life force energy, not personal energy. Some of these modalities include Reiki, Qigong, Pranic healing, prayer, meditation, guided visualization, sound and light healing, as well as aromatherapy.

When I conduct individual healing sessions and group meditation, I utilize guided visualization, focusing on the patient's intention to heal themselves. Through 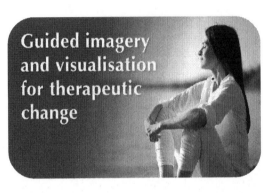 guided visualization and intention, I assist my patients to release their spiritual, psychological, and physiological barriers, both conscious and subconscious, that prevent them from healing.

By releasing spiritual, physiological, and psychological barriers and blocks, a person can create a healing environment within their mind, body, and spirit, unlocking their power to heal. During healing sessions, my intention is to reach mental stillness aligned with God's source and Divine will, including seeing a person's wholeness so the individual can undergo complete healing.

Through several spiritual experiences, I was summoned to work with patients, commit to embodying wholeness, and continue the self-care practice I have implemented throughout my life.

During my healing practices, I can support my patients with empathy, compassion, and a deep sense of unconditional love because of my commitment to embodying and honoring the wholeness of the human mind, body, and spirit. The degree of success through energetic healing depends on the patient's mindset and desire to be healed. The transfer of healing energy is site-specific. The patient must have a positive mindset and a strong desire to be healed. This will determine their level of success in restoring their body's natural flow of energy, thus facilitating self-healing.

THE HEALING SESSION

Many people in the world are carrying heavy amounts of negative, hindering, and destructive energetic loads with them. Spiritual healing is effective for anyone who is willing to let go of this weight. Anyone can be healed, including people with psychiatric conditions such as depression, anxiety, stress, PTSD, and trauma. People with chronic medical conditions can also be healed. The possibilities are limitless if the individual is committed to their own healing journey.

The actual healing session is administered by placing hands close to a patient's body. The healer projects by thought and utilization

of electromagnetic energy to the patient. This method of healing can also be done through distance. Energy or subtler universal forms are accelerated during the process of healing. The energy associated with recovery may be outside the known electromagnetic spectrum, unrecognized by medical science. Illness and disease are a result of imbalances in the normal flow of a healthy body.

The majority of healing modalities only work with specific systems and not the entire body. For instance, biofeedback works mainly with pain management but not our whole body or spiritual being. Spiritual healing provides a unique opportunity that gives the body a chance to heal from a specific illness and provides a pathway of energetic, physical, and emotional healing, which contributes to total wellness.

During a spiritual healing session, the practitioner and the patient can experience a multitude of sensations and side effects, some pleasant and others unusual. Even the unique sensations and side effects indicate healing as the patient is releasing old, heavy, and negative energy. Clearing out old energies is imperative for welcoming the new energy. There is a shift taking place; harmony is being found.

Some of the sensations and side effects experienced include tingling, bubbling, numbness, feeling cold and hot, fatigue, exhaustion, and mood swings. Physical energy surges are also experienced, where individuals feel the release or movement of energy within their body.

The deeper the healer can go, and the more receptive the patient is to receiving universal life force energy, the greater the chances of healing becomes. Even the most skeptical of individuals can experience spiritual healing if they allow for it.

ENERGY CENTERS AND PATHWAYS

The human body, as mentioned, is made up of trillions of electrically charged cells, all interacting and communicating with one another. There is a complex energy system inside of us. The body has several energy centers and pathways (pictured), broken down into the Etheric body, and the four lower bodies of energy: the  Etheric Body, the Emotional, the Mental Body, and the Physical Body. These bodies are a physical presence that each have their own unique blockages contained within. If aligned and functioning properly, these bodies can have tremendous power to do good with the help of God. If they work together as one, you can more easily feel the presence of God in your life. The tools within this book will help to identify, clear, and return each body to balance, which will in turn will help you progress and advance on the spiritual path.

The Etheric Body serves as the energy system for the physical body. It is the energy system humans are most associated with. The Etheric body connects us with God's energy itself, and is much less individualized than the other bodies. Inside the Etheric Body, there are three categories of energy: Nadis, Chakras, and Auras.

There are 72,000 Nadis (pictured) in the physical body. These are tiny energy channels that communicate and send universal life force energy throughout the body to the emotional body's Chakras, different from the seven chakras of the emotional body. The chakras then send energy back to the Nadis in a loop-like system; energy is continually circulated throughout the physical body.

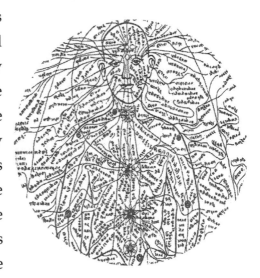

The Emotional Body, also referred to as the Astral Body, serves as the energy system for the emotional body, containing the Seven Primary Chakras. The astral body delivers energy to the chakras so that an individual can have and store emotional experiences – ranging the entire spectrum of pleasurable to unpleasable, from trauma to desire. The Astral body is critical to the human experience. It generates context and meaning in the experiences we have throughout our life. When humans suppress emotions, they block the flow of life energy and create anxiety, stress, and unpleasant emotions. The Astral Body also emits an Aura, which is your personal energy field.

Your auric energy fields complete your energy anatomy. Everyone has an aura surrounding them, which connects your energy to universal energy. It can be visualized with seven distinct layers reflecting various aspects of your body, mind, and spirit. The colors of auras may change, reflecting your current physical, emotional, mental, or spiritual state of being.

During a spiritual healing session, the healer's aura is often powerful. The healer's aura brightens with golden light, representing the spiritual light from God channeling through them. God's light forms an energy field around and within the healer, emanating from their hands and encompassing the patient in a beautiful bubble of light. This is a sign that the healing process is in effect.

The Mental Body serves as the energy system for the mental component of the human body. Within the Mental Body, there are two parts, the Mental and Causal fields.

The Mental field holds information like the proper function of biological processes and systems and our general intelligence and higher intelligence. The Causal field, also referred to as the Karmic Body, comprises our karmic history and all action we have taken throughout our life. Our belief system can also be found in the Causal body.

These energy centers and pathways throughout the human body provide a vital link between the body, mind, spiritual bodies, Etheric, Astral, and Mental. An imbalance or blockage in any of the energy bodies can result in a disease process getting a foothold, which manifests as a symptom or "warning sign." When this happens, the universal life force energy running through the body is obstructed and can result in physical or mental illness, emotional and spiritual imbalances, and reduced overall vitality.

SPIRITUAL HEALING AS A COMPLEMENTARY COMPONENT TO CONVENTIONAL MEDICINE

The only way to achieve "true healing" is to learn how to control the total body with someone experienced in the field and has been trained to heal, such as an energy healer. An energy healer can help patients align their energy pathways and teach them how to balance the body since they have often already accomplished this. Spiritual healing must be added to our emotional wellness program and not meant to replace other medicine areas but to compliment them and assist us in transforming and healing ourselves from within. According to the National Federation of Spiritual Healers (NFSH), spiritual healing is a "natural energy therapy that complements conventional medicine by treating the whole person, mind, body, emotions, spirit, and soul. Healers act as a conduit for healing energy. The benefits of which can be felt on many levels, including the physical."

Spiritual healing, amongst other alternative approaches to healing, complements conventional medicine in many ways. Allopathic medicine practitioners are starting to embrace alternative healing methods. More research and studies are conducted on these healing techniques. The research is not vast, but it is growing as alternative healing methods gain more and more popularity worldwide.

Everyone has the same goal, which is to be healthy. As spiritual healing becomes a more mainstream approach to healing, I believe we will witness a dramatic change in people's overall health and happiness. Including positive effects and changes such as increased energy, clear thinking, the manifestation of abundance, better sleep, ample amounts of joy, healthier relationships, and overall improved complete health, spiritual healing is well on its way to healing many.

There are many basic principles of spiritual healing, which are common to all practices. However, you must realize that everything in the world consists of energy, including people. Every type of physical matter is composed of vibrating strands of energy. When two objects or human beings vibrate at different energies close to each other, their energy adapts. They begin to become associated and exhibit the same vibration or resonance. This is why the spiritual healer and the client must be partners in the spiritual healing process. The practitioner channels the energy while the client draws the energy provided into their body. Thus, all healing is ultimately self-healing. Spiritual healing exists to serve the highest and greatest good of all parties involved.

Sources:

https://energyhealinginstitute.org (Energy Bodies)

https://susanjamieson.com/quantum-healing/energetic-healing-side-effects/ (Sensations, side effects, and benefits)

https://www.mayoclinic.org/tests-procedures/complementary-alternative-medicine/in-depth/alternative-medicine/art-20045267 (complimentary to allopathic medicine)

Etheric Body: http://www.mindoverimage.com/wp-content/uploads/2017/02/600_434270158.jpeg

Astral Body: https://energie-sante.net/images/imgeh/EH160_nadis-01.jpg

CHAPTER 2
PHYSICAL BARRIERS TO HEALTH

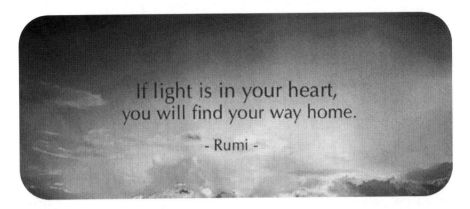

If light is in your heart,
you will find your way home.

- Rumi -

A short while back, a 72-year-old woman called me, seeking healing. This lovely woman, Melissa, was a prolific writer and published author. She had been diagnosed with stage four uterine cancer four years prior and had been suffering ever since. When Melissa reached out to me, cancer had metastasized to her organs, including her liver, adrenals, and significant blood vessel.

She was severely ill and in severe pain. Melissa wanted to be healed; however, cancer had spread so significantly that the possibility of physical healing was unlikely and nearly impossible. I informed her that her physical body was considerably compromised. It would be challenging to perform healing on her physical body in the state it was in. Spiritual healing can rarely change the physical body's biochemistry after an illness as intense and damaging to the body as stage four cancers have metastasized to vital organs for nearly four years.

I wanted to assist Melissa in her healing; however, I would not undo the damage that had already been done. The state her body was in was itself a physical barrier to healing. Cancer had started to deteriorate her body, so I decided to focus my healing abilities on Melissa's spiritual and psychological healing.

The cancer was not only compromising the health of Melissa's physical body, but it was also compromising her psychological and spiritual health as well. The pain and severity of cancer led Melissa to psychological agony.

Melissa consulted a medium to address her curiosities and deep-seated fears over the unknown concept of death before reaching out to me. Melissa was raised Jewish, so her understanding and beliefs around death varied. The medium and I provided comfort for Melissa, informing her that she would be met by God, her dearest loved ones that passed on, and beautiful angelic beings after death.

Melissa still did not want to die. She was in denial regarding her life situation and felt angry at God for giving her what she saw as a cruel burden. As many people are, Melissa was afraid to die. She was also angry at God because she felt she had not yet lived a full life. Death was not something she considered at her age.

Melissa's parents died at age 90, so her understanding and experience related to death were that someone age 72 was too young to experience something as conclusive as death! Melissa also informed me of her traumatic history of physical abuse she endured by her mother and sexual abuse by her Father.

After listening to Melissa, I knew she needed to release the negative emotions she was carrying inside her. This would allow her to find comfort and peace during the dying process.

Melissa and I discussed different options. I told her that I would provide comfort for her in the dying process, assisting with psychological and spiritual healing to release the negative emotions perpetuating her pain. I encouraged Melissa to forgive God, her parents, and herself. Then release the anger and resentment she held to experience inner peace, promoting spiritual and psychological harmony throughout her body.

I told Melissa that she would be rewarded for her life of service as a college professor who taught internationally. Her writings empower women in profound ways. Melissa was also a mentor and support system for female entrepreneurs, including myself! She was a woman of service on this beautiful planet and was always more than willing and happy to help others.

People like Melissa are rewarded dramatically once they leave this realm, mostly when they have lived out their soul's mission. As I shared this information with Melissa, she expressed a sigh of relief. Melissa allowed herself to let go of her resentment towards God during our healing sessions. She was able to receive God's energy.

Melissa became at peace with the dying process and knew that she would meet her Higher Powers after death, which instilled peace and love within her. While Melissa's physical body could not be healed through spiritual healing because of her condition. I helped Melissa create a state of inner peace, acceptance, and unconditional love. She left the physical plane entered the astral plane on Thanksgiving. Melissa's beautiful spirit lives on forever. The spirit never dies.

"Die happily and look forward to taking up a new and better form. Like the sun, only when you set in the west you can rise in the east." – Rumi

Illness is usually a message from the universe that change may be needed in your life.

Many people think that medical science or their physician has all the answers to healing the body when illness prevails. Suppose a physician tells an individual that they have cancer. In that case, they can view the diagnosis as something to fear or make the lifestyle or emotional changes needed.

The individual and their health care professional then go on a journey to uncover the events that led to their illness. Speaking with a healer or physician can discover secrets that encompass many factors. These include poor dietary choices, alcohol, drug usage, reducing stress, or changing negative habits.

The use of prayer, visualization, and meditation can help those needing to make changes, especially where conflict has been unresolved or the type always giving to others and allowing little time for them, resulting in resentment being accumulated. They can be on the path of loving themselves more fully and then allowing the spontaneous change of allowing God to heal them.

Healing of an injury responds typically to two factors. First, the body's condition and how the natural healing energy can react in a positive nature.

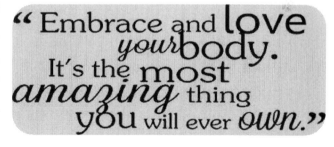
"Embrace and love your body. It's the most amazing thing you will ever own."

Second is the mental attitude concerning the illness? I have observed patients that heal faster than others with similar diseases. Analyzing the reasons, I came to several conclusions.

One of the more significant reasons is that negativity is present. This results in the person's lack of flexibility of mind and inability to allow the healing forces to enter. This negativity will also slow the healing process.

A healthy body and internal organs, when in optimum health, possess a natural harmony or vibration. The mind plays a vital role in holding onto negativity. When you hold onto negativity in the form of resentment, anger, despair, or conflict, the body cannot heal itself. Controlling negativity allows every part of the body, controlled by the mind, to collaborate and coordinate with every cell to become involved in the healing process.

Loving your body activates your immune system to generate an aura of kindness, forgiveness, and unconditional love towards others so you can be blessed. It is in choosing this unconditional love for your body that allows the force of life and healing to surround you.

PHYSICAL REASONS FOR NOT HEALING

There are several physical barriers to healing. A physical barrier does not rule out the possibility of spiritual healing altogether. However, physical barriers make the healing process more arduous. They require more time, a greater desire to heal, and a strong belief in their own powers to self-heal.

Some of these physical barriers include inadequate nutrition, certain medications, poor blood circulation, being overweight, preexisting health conditions, and more severe diagnoses such as metastatic cancer, cardiovascular disease, Alzheimer's disease, dementia, Parkinson's disease, and Multiple Sclerosis. There are miraculous testimonies of people who have completely healed, gone into remission, and regressed some of the most intense physical barriers.

16

People who are blind can see that people who are paralyzed can walk. People with Parkinson's experience a complete reversal of lost movement and sensation. People diagnosed with stage four cancers go into remission all through different spiritual modalities of healing. I would be mistaken to say certain conditions cannot be healed.

However, nothing is impossible if willpower and receptivity are there, even when the barriers and obstacles seem unconquerable.

PREVENTIVE MEASURES

Adequate nutrition is a lot more important than people may think. Healthy eating is one of the best practices for preventing illness and disease. Nourishing your body with whole foods, eating a balanced diet consisting of mostly plant-based products, and doing so while you are healthy! Many people face that they are not focused on eating healthy foods until they absolutely have to, until eating healthy becomes literally a do or die situation.

Eating healthy is an underestimated factor and rarely discussed between a physician and patient. Diet is discussed when a patient sees the physician for a diet-related health condition, such as heart disease, diabetes, obesity, high blood pressure, etc. Otherwise, diet is typically overlooked. Providing the body with proper nutrition is vital. Your body is the only body you have right now, so why not treat it that way?

The body is a remarkably sacred vessel that holds your very life. This is an important reminder for us all. Why put anything into the body that will not be of the highest quality to do well for the body? Your body is in a delicate balance between health and illness.

Foods like meat, wheat, refined sugar, eggs, dairy, and processed foods cause your body to produce acid. Studies show that eating more alkaline foods can protect the body from becoming more acidic. The body's pH (acid/base balance) is tightly regulated. It is continually working to balance chemical levels. It is difficult to change the body's pH levels; nevertheless, eating alkaline-rich foods will help maintain them more efficiently.

Most fruits and vegetables are alkaline, promoting foods.

 Some of the best alkaline fruits and vegetables include spinach, kale, beets, figs, avocado, and cucumber. More alkaline foods include seeds, nuts, legumes, soybeans, and tofu. There are several diets to choose from on the market, such as the very trendy alkaline diet, intermittent fasting, ketogenic, Mediterranean, vegetarian, or plant-based.

I'm going to change the word "diet" to "lifestyle" since eating healthy is not a 30-day challenge or meant to last for only a brief period of your life; eating healthy should be integrated into your everyday lifestyle. No matter which lifestyle of food you choose to incorporate into your life, maintaining a healthy balance is the key.

Lastly, developing a positive and loving relationship between you and your food is crucial. Remember, your body is sacred. Feeding yourself nourishing foods is an act of love for your body and creates a balanced and healthy internal environment. Some simple lifestyle changes incorporate into your daily life that promotes a healthy gut (home of your immune system).

Consuming probiotics is one of those changes. You can get probiotics by drinking a mixture of boiled apple cider vinegar (1 tsp) and fresh ginger daily. Teas are great ways to flush and detox the intestines.

Remember, 70-80% of your immune system is in your gut – it must be kept healthy. As you age, your immune system gradually loses the ability to optimally protect the body. Adding supplements to your daily routine is fundamental to maximize the effectiveness of your immune system. Some of these critical supplements include vitamin D3, zinc, vitamin C, and B vitamins, including B12 and B6.

Be sure to cook with quality oils such as coconut, Ghee, or olive oil. Keep fried foods at a minimum, and consume an adequate level of Omega 3 fatty acids such as walnuts and flaxseed. Also, consuming superfoods, such as green leafy vegetables, seeds, and berries, and drinking plenty of water every day to flush toxins and aid in digestive health.

YOGIC BENEFITS

Yoga is one of the oldest known methods of improving and sustaining a healthy, functional body. It is a practice that unites the mind, body, and spirit. Yoga has an abundant number of benefits, physical benefits making up just a small percentage of all the ways yoga improves one's wellbeing.

Some of the physical benefits include, but are not limited to, managing and reducing stress, lowering blood pressure, regulating the heart rate, improving cardio and circulatory health, raising energy and core frequencies, easing joint pain, and improving strength, balance, flexibility. All of these benefits can also result in slowing the aging process. Yoga is a practice that unites the mind, body, and spirit.

Yogic practices are varied. Physical posture helps balance your endocrine system. It will also energize your Pranic energy centers (no-touch healing system) and breathing exercises to further regulate and optimize the body's overall health.

We will discuss more yogic benefits and their goodness in  both the spiritual barriers to healing chapter and the psychological barriers to healing chapter. Yoga is the most complete form of exercise, integrating healing mind, body, and spirit techniques amongst the countless different practice styles.

STEM CELLS - THE DAWNING OF A NEW AGE OF MEDICINE

We are literally in the infancy of a medical breakthrough that will not only extend life but may also cure most diseases. This medical breakthrough may have the key to unlock longevity, as well. What is this breakthrough? Stem cells and their regenerative properties. Stem cells are the cells in our body that replace damaged, dead, or old cells, but we currently only have a limited supply. To maintain the stem cells we have, nutrition is the key.

Proper nutrition and living an active lifestyle provide support to these unique and invaluable cells. Stem cells are in limited supply for the time being, so keeping them healthy is critically important. In recent years, stem cell science has sky-rocketed into the public domain with information astounding to all scientific community areas.

Current uses for stem cells is in bone marrow transplant patients whose stem cells have been damaged or destroyed during chemotherapy or radiation therapy for cancer. At the rate science is advancing, we may be able to utilize the cells in the event of illness to heal our bodies or even replace a damaged organ. Stem cell nutrition will be an important area of wellness in the 21st century.

Stem Cell

CHAPTER 3
SPIRITUAL TOOLS FOR HEALING

Throughout my practice, I've worked with patients who heal slower – if they heal at all than others with similar ailments. I've noted a pattern in these individuals. It wasn't that they couldn't heal, except for a few cases where their physical symptoms had progressed to a terminal point. Also, they had a blockage, physical, psychological, or spiritual, which prevented them from being able to heal.

Illness is usually a message from the universe that change may be needed in your life. Many people think that medical science or the physician has all the answers regarding healing the body when illness prevails. Suppose a physician tells an individual that they have cancer. In that case, they can view the diagnosis as something to fear or make the lifestyle or emotional changes needed.

The individual and their health care professional then go on a journey to uncover the events that led to their illness. In this approach, by speaking with their healer or physician, they can discover some of those secrets that can encompass a multitude of factors such as poor dietary choices, alcohol use, drug use, or changing negative other habits.

The use of prayer, visualization, and meditation can help those needing to make changes, especially where conflict has been unresolved or the type always giving to others and allowing little time for them, resulting in resentment being accumulated.

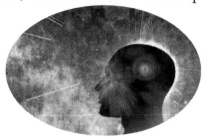

They can be on the path of loving themselves more fully and then allowing the spontaneous change of allowing God to heal them. One such woman I worked with, who we'll call Jessica, came to me after being diagnosed with breast cancer. In her late 40s, it was clear she was a beautiful soul, kind, and compassionate. Still, the darkness that sat just behind her eyes was impossible to ignore.

She harbored immense amounts of resentment and anger at God for cursing her with such an awful condition. It was as though she'd already decided that she was going to die and that there was nothing more she could do about it. Yet here she was, coming to me for spiritual healing.

With the rise of so-called "rational thought" in our industry, technological era, spiritual healing has become a taboo practice. The focus of these modern practices is to respond to symptoms rather than trying to root the problem out from the source. Many Western medical practitioners viewed, and still consider, the proven efficacy of spiritual interventions as nothing more than a placebo effect from so-called woo-woo rituals.

Before we go any further, I would like to point out how counterintuitive that train of thought actually is. We know the power of the placebo effect. A patient will even begin to heal themselves by simply believing a treatment is working. That fact alone should be enough to prove the power of intention, of accepting healing as the first and most effective step toward being healed. The spiritual and the physical are not two entirely separate and isolated spheres, as western medicine might have you believe. Instead, the two playoffs each other, a push and a pull, a give and take as all things are.

The positive gain will also be "risk-free" and is a non-invasive treatment. Rarely at times, the practitioner will touch the patient but can provide additional support in their medical or surgical history. All physical troubles, in one way or another, have at their center a spiritual origin.

Initially, they will manifest as a minute physical ailment, such as chest pains, sore throats, headaches, or manageable psychological ones such as depression, anxiety, or PTSD. Suppose these go unresolved or are only treated with symptom alleviating solutions using painkillers. In that case, they will almost inevitably result in more permanent or severe problems.

To disregard the spiritual side entirely in favor of the purely physical is to cut off a tree's dying branch while ignoring the infected, rotted core. The use of complementary or spiritual healing can and should have a role in traditional medicine. Many physicians regard spiritual healing as being unproven. However, many are also seeing that spiritual healing does assist with a wide variety of illnesses. There appears to be a need to place spiritual healing in a better light or more substantial ground in the medical community.

> The natural healing force within each one of us is the greatest force in getting well.
>
> - Hippocrates

Western societies are becoming increasingly more interested in using complementary medicine practices for themselves. They are utilizing these practices more each day. There is no guarantee of spiritual healing when it comes to treating people. Still, there is no such guarantee with medical intervention either. However, in utilizing spiritual healing, the patient most likely spends more time with a spiritual practitioner and will be listened to more carefully than when seen by a conventional medical provider.

If nothing else, they will gain benefits on mental, emotional, and spiritual levels if not on the physical level. And as we said before, the human mind is a powerful tool. With that knowledge, it's become even clearer to see why spiritual healing has been practiced in nearly every culture worldwide throughout history.

And why Jessica, now at the end of her metaphorical rope, chose to come to me to heal problems that hadn't been resolved by western medicine alone. As Jessica and I began to work together, it became clear that this anger and resentment she held for the universe did not start with her diagnosis. Jessica had never been a particularly religious individual. However, as a child of two non-practicing Christian parents, she had a fundamental belief that God was controlling the goings-on of the universe.

Without the ability to understand how a loving God could allow the world to exist the way it has, Jessica developed anxiety and depression. A life full of suffering, and she always seemed to be on the receiving end, which had become unbearable. She resented the God she believed was there but who didn't care about her.

This diagnosis was, understandably, and was the straw that broke the camel's back. How could a loving God only stack this as the malignant cherry on top? Given everything she'd experienced in her life, it made sense she couldn't heal. She'd never been able to heal from those old emotional and spiritual wounds. Therefore how could she possibly begin to heal from these new physical ones?

There's reason to believe that all the old unresolved emotional and spiritual issues lying dormant within her subconscious played a role, however small, in manifesting this physical ailment. These issues, mind you, could very well stretch much farther back than Jessica might even be aware of. Though yes, she had unresolved traumatic experiences within this physical incarnation. They are only a symptom of a more extensive series of unresolved spiritual, karmic wounds.

Karma

Though the idea of karma has been warped in Western New Age tradition, at its core is a cycle of cause and effect.

From the ancient Egyptian concept of ma'at to the Greek heimarmene to the Germanic wyrd, every major culture has bad karma. The Sanskrit word we all know as karma translates roughly to "action." It does not behave as many in the west have been taught to believe. Such as a bank balance of good and bad deeds that immediately return within days, weeks, or months, but instead spanning across whole lifetimes.

Karma is the sum of a person's actions in this and previous states of existence, which decide their fate in future realities. These prior actions manifest everything from social status, to familial placement, to the physical and psychological state of being. In the East, karma is accepted by almost everyone, as it is a central pillar of both Buddhism and Hinduism. In Hinduism, karma fundamentally structures day-to-day life, believing that one's past life's collective actions are what causes them to be born into a Jati. This community determines one's role in society.

How people treat you is their karma; how you react is yours.

Karma manifests in the Buddhist tradition similarly. One who is born in their next incarnation of Samsara, or the cycle of rebirth, determined by one's past action, rather than the actions themselves. Samsara only stops when the individual reaches Nirvana or Moksha, also known as enlightenment.

Karma is a fundamental aspect of many Eastern societies. Individuals born into them believe their spiritual growth comes from within, rather than from an external divine force such as God or Jesus, as many modern Abrahamic traditions have taught. Judaism, Christianity, and Islam held a belief in karma.

However, the concept was removed from the practice somewhere in the fifth century as the church became more of a political entity than a spiritual one. However, we do see the remnants of the concept in 2 Corinthians 9:6, "Whoever sows sparingly will also reap sparingly, and whoever sows generously will also reap generously." Galatians 6:7, "Do not be deceived: God cannot be mocked. A man reaps what he sows."

At their core, all forms of religious mysticism say the same thing: we all must, as souls, learn compassion toward others, right action, purity of mind, and service to humanity. And through that, can we find healing for ourselves. Though the path may differ for each religion (and even more so for each individual), they all lead towards the glorious mountaintop.

Karma is not a punishment or an excuse to blame others, but a complex learning process to assist you in your soul growth. We establish our own life purpose with an individualized set of lessons and goals before we ever choose to incarnate in these physical bodies. The soul decides with God the plan of the enfoldment of their life. Unresolved grudges or wounds in one lifetime will manifest themselves in similar ways, either in this lifetime or the next – and then the next after that, if still unresolved.

Karmic cycles can hinder your spiritual evolution to such a degree that karmic cleansing is needed to expand consciousness. This is why identifying, accepting, and resolving karmic cycles are essential to healing. Knowing you are a spiritual being, the creator of your own life  circumstances, you can release and clear emotional or behavioral patterns from your past.

Once you have resolved the source of your karmic imbalance, you can begin to return to equilibrium. Then to the natural state of universal balance of love and surrender that is your birthright.

Only then can healing genuinely manifest. Now, talking about it is all well and good, but how does one identify these karmic cycles? Well, one way is to simply look at your life for repeating problems either with family, relationships (romantic or otherwise), or even in the way you speak to yourself. Sometimes it can really as simple as doing some introspection.

In Jessica's case, resentment towards God's apathy about her life circumstances pushed her further away from being able to accept the cycles and lessons her soul had chosen explicitly for her. Her inability to forgive and trust God, or by extension, forgive and trust in herself, was a cycle she had been trapped in her entire life. And most likely the lifetimes that preceded this one.

In other instances, there are much larger issues known as Generational Curses. According to the Gospel, a generational curse describes the cumulative effect and consequence on a person of their ancestor's actions, beliefs, and sins being passed down. Similarly, we can identify patterns of behavior passed down from our parents, their parents before them, and so on, which are unhealthy and detrimental to our emotional and spiritual wellbeing.

There is also scientific evidence supporting this, showing that massively traumatic events affect a survivor's lineage's DNA. A study of epigenetic shows lower cortisol levels (a hormone that regulates stress levels), leading to higher rates of PTSD in the descendants of holocaust survivors. This despite the fact they are not the ones who endured it.

While we may not have been the direct cause of our own suffering or even the ones who directly experienced trauma itself, we are the ones who have to deal with it, one way or the other. Identifying what cause it can lead us towards the path of healing.

The more challenging part that follows is forgiving ourselves or others for our roles in these cycles. Since they can appear so obvious and/or avoidable once we do identify them. However, by holding onto these feelings of anger, guilt, or a lack of forgiveness, we only proliferate the issues we were trying to solve in the first place. The first step towards healing any long-lasting emotional wound is accepting things as they are, not for how they should have been.

We live in the present moment, not the past or the future. But that doesn't mean that we don't play a role in creating our own reality. Reinhold Niebuhr's Serenity Prayer is a perfect tool to aid us as we work through the process of healing ourselves.

God, grant me the serenity to accept the things I cannot change. And courage to change the things I can, and wisdom to know the difference.

Understanding that there are things out of our control and becoming at peace allows us to surrender to the loving guidance the universe provides for us. Realize and accepting there are things out of our control that simultaneously come into clarity. There is only one thing we truly have control over, which is ourselves. We can control what we put out into the world, and we should always aim towards love, compassion, and forgiveness.

In Hawaiian culture, it was believed that illness could not be cured until the person atoned for their transgressions, which is why they became ill in the first place. They must work with a priest to overcome the problem and receive forgiveness from their entire family. The following prayer is Ho'oponopono, the Hawaiian prayer for forgiveness. It's a simple prayer, done by the repetition of these four phrases.

After our first meeting, I offered these two practices to Jessica. Though she was initially wary of it, never having been one for prayer or meditation, she agreed. To convince her, I recited my favorite Mark Twain quote: "If you do what you have always done, you will get what you have always got." The only thing she had to lose was nothing.

There are no downsides to trying these practices other than your own judgment and lack of acceptance. If they don't work for you, at least you can say you tried. The next time I saw her, two weeks later, it had clearly had an effect. Though it was still there, however, the darkness in her eyes had lightened, giving way to the loving and compassionate nature that is her true, higher self.

This practice is incredibly similar to Eastern forms of meditation that have recently become so popular in the West. Namely, the Ho'oponopono is most similar to Metta Bhavana, or loving-kindness meditation. The steps to loving-kindness meditation may seem simple but can be surprisingly difficult as it progresses. This practice can be as long or short as you want it to be, but the practice's repetition is the most crucial part. Just like anything else, these types of self-work don't happen overnight. It proceeds as such:

1. Find somewhere peaceful and quiet, where you will not be disturbed. Set a timer for however long you intend to practice.

   The timer will prevent your conscious mind from worrying about how much time you're spending in this practice.

2. Sit or lie down, comfortable but alert. Relax your muscles. Focus on taking deep, slow, even breaths.

3. Imagine yourself in a state of pure, unfiltered physical and emotional wellness and inner peace. Try to cultivate a feeling of unconditional love for yourself, be grateful, and accept all your perceived flaws. Since they are what make you, you, and you are perfect just as you are.

4. Repeat the phrases; *May I be happy. May I be safe, May I be healthy, peaceful, and strong. May I give and receive unconditional love today.*

Some individuals may choose to replace "May I" with "I AM," as in God said to Moses, "I AM THAT I AM." This I AM consciousness is the Christ Consciousness or Nirvana, the higher self that is the state of pure being or is-ness. This ideology behind the extremely popular I AM affirmations is used by millionaires and artists. The daily practice of writing down phrases such as "I AM smart" or "I AM beautiful" or "I AM filled with love" embodying the reality you want to manifest.

If your mind starts to drift, gently try to redirect it back towards these feelings of loving-kindness. Repeat these four phrases, really embodying these feelings during your practice for a few days.

The next step is to focus these feelings on someone you care deeply about a spouse, a child, a parent, or a best friend. Replace the "I" in the fourth step with their name. If your biggest struggle is forgiving and loving you, it might be most comfortable to start with this step first and then move on to yourself.

Once you've completed the first stages of Loving Kindness, Meditation with yourself and/or your loved ones, then move on to someone you feel more neutral about, such as a coworker, a classmate, a stranger you passed on the street. Repeat the process. Then repeat with a person, you have negative feelings towards a boss, an ex, a political figure.

By conditioning yourself to extend this same loving compassion towards these individuals, you might find yourself diametrically opposed in every regard. You are developing unconditional love and compassion for every being on this planet, which are all you, and you are all them. And if you can love them, there's no reason you can't love yourself.

This compassion and loving understanding will allow you to let go of any old cycles and bring you back to that state of balance from which physical healing can occur. As a nation and planet, we face many uncertainties. One of the vital spiritual tools we can call upon is prayer. Just as with meditation, prayer is a focus of intention and energy to manifest a specific outcome. Unlike Eastern meditation, prayer is a communication between oneself and God. However, it is essential to remember that God is within us, as we are all divine beings.

Some people can spontaneously say flowing words from their hearts, but others find great comfort at times like these with traditional prayers that have stood the test of time. One of the most well-known prayers in the West is the Lord's Prayer since it has that familiar rhythm that many of us can recite by rote without focusing on the meaning.

Though Jessia did find comfort in the Ho'oponopono, since it was a newer, less familiar practice for her, it didn't sink in immediately. When I suggested utilizing this translation of "Our father from Aramaic" by Neil Douglas-Klotz, she connected with it on a much deeper level.

It's not that one practice is better or more effective overall than another; it will only resonate most deeply with the individual. The Lord's Prayer is one of Jesus' central teachings. It is about our relationship with God and others, and perhaps it's worth a more in-depth look. Jesus spoke the ancient language of Aramaic, a "cousin" of Hebrew.

By the time the New Testament got recorded, it was in Greek, then Latin, and much later, English. The English version begins:

"Our father who art in heaven" in Aramaic, the word used is abwoon, which means Divine Parent. Like God, it's genderless. But it also means *The Oneness, Creative flow of Blessing, the breath of the Holy Spirit, and the vibration from the Holy Spirit as it touches and interpenetrates form. Heaven in Aramaic presents the image of light and sound shining through all of creation.*

In translation, you recite *O Thou! The Breathing Life of all, Creator of the Shimmering Sound that touches us.*

"Hallowed by thy name" becomes: *Help us breathe one holy breath feeling only you-this creates a shrine inside, in wholeness.*

34

Here Jesus reminds us of our Divine nature that God resides inside of us. Therein lays our wholeness, no matter what the body's eyes see.

"**Thy kingdom come**" is the next line. In Aramaic: *Desire with and through us the rule of universal fruitfulness onto the earth. He could just as easily have said: Come into the bedroom of our hearts, prepare us for the marriage of power and beauty.*

Either way, we are looking at how we co-create and pro-create in partnership with God. God gives us the vision and brings it to fruitfulness through the desire placed in our hearts.

"**Thy will be done in earth, as it is in heaven.**" In Aramaic: *Create in me a divine cooperation-from many selves, one voice, and one action. This also translates, quite poetically, as: Let all wills move together in your vortex, as stars and planets swirl through the sky.*

We get the sense of both the unity and diversity in the Oneness of all God's creation.

"**Give us this day our daily bread**" expands into *Grant what we need each day in bread and insight; substance for the call of growing life.*

But it just as easily could be: Animate the earth within us: we then feel the Wisdom underneath supporting all. This is why it doesn't stop at daily bread; we get wisdom and insight as well.

"**And forgive us our debts, as we forgive our debtors**" translates into: *Erase the inner marks our failures make, just as we scrub our hearts of others' faults.*

I love the image of scrubbing our hearts of other's faults. Notice the subtlety here. Sin also translates as accidental offenses or tangled threads. The more immense harm is the judging of actions and forgetting the divinity of ourselves and others. In our

Oneness, there are no us "versus" them. In our Oneness, there is just one heart.

"**And lead us not into temptation, but deliver us from evil,**" becomes: *Deceived neither by the outer nor the inner-free us to walk your path with joy.*

In the Aramaic, no one leads us into temptation, least of all, God. The word temptation becomes a much less charged distraction. The point is to get back, not too self-righteous piety, but to a joyous partnership with God.

The prayer ends: "**For Thine is the Kingdom, & the Power, & the Glory, forever, Amen.**" In Aramaic, it's: *From you is born all ruling will, the power and life to do, the song that beautifies all from age to age it renews.*

Using this version of the prayer brings forth much more of the spiritual essence it holds, rather than merely reciting the syllables from memory. Though words themselves do have power, connecting to the language on a deeper level, a more fundamental, spiritual level, evoking the healing power of love.

Also, most of Jessica's church experiences were not entirely positive. She could use this alternate translation to realign herself with her own relationship to her faith.

By connecting to the meaning, she could see past and forgive the human fallibility of her experiences to the divine perfection that is love. With any of these practices, you can complement them very well using what Theosophists call the Violet Flame. Within every person's heart, there is a core of violet-colored flame. It can be used to transmute energies we perceive to be negative into positive, loving energies.

This process is available when you set your intention to do it. All you need to do is focus on the energy you wish to remove.

Then use your intentions and practice to transmute them into a higher vibrational, more compassionate energy.

Using these practices, with psychotherapy, will complement the allopathic treatment Jessica was undergoing. Her ability to forgive herself, her parents, and God allowed her to realign herself with the unconditional love of the universe and truly begin to heal on not just emotional and spiritual levels but physical as well. By accepting these healing modalities, she's massively improved her quality of life, relationship with herself and has since gone into remission.

The last time I saw her, there was still a hint of that darkness in her eyes, but it was vastly outshined by the love and compassion that I always saw was there.

The Lords Prayer

Our Father who art in Heaven
hallowed be thy name.
Thy kingdom come, thy will be done,
on earth as it is in Heaven.
Give us this day our daily bread
and forgive us our trespasses,
as we forgive those who trespass against us.
Lead us not into temptation
but deliver us from evil.
For thine is the kingdom, the power
and the glory, for ever and ever.
Amen

CHAPTER 4
THE POWER OF THE MIND TO HEAL

Can we manifest optimum health? Proponents of the law of attraction, mind metaphysics, and other traditional mind-body schools believe so. The testimonies of success from using the power of mind are endless: financial abundance, positive career changes, loving relationships, and of course, restoration of health. There are no limits to what we can accomplish using the mind, along with the power of the spirit.

Chiropractor turned self-help teacher Dr. Joe Dispenza openly details the accounts of putting his spine back together following a tragic bicycling accident. Doctors told Joe that he would never walk again without a risky and experimental surgery, to which he declined. He now documents cases of spontaneous self-healing occurring within the walls of his retreats. Everything from MS, vision impairment to mental trauma are overturned on the spot, and the list goes on.

Aside from its scientific documentation, there is nothing new about healing ourselves with our minds. Several studies regarding the Placebo effect show that simply believing or expecting to be healed (or harmed) by something appearing to be a medical treatment can, in fact, lead to that desired outcome.

Believe it or not, spontaneous healing is a part of our culture and has been with us since the beginning. It is found within all of our religious and spiritual traditions, going back to Jesus. He was accounted for creating many miraculous healings throughout his lifetime. Of course, Jesus was the son of God, but that same God and His power to heal lay inside of each one of us.

The basis of mind metaphysics says that we are all pieces of the whole One Infinite God, that our mind is His mind, and that we can tap into His powers inside.

WHAT DO WE MEAN BY MANIFESTATION?

"Be still and know I am God."

What do we mean exactly when we talk about the power of the mind to manifest? The simplest way to understand it is that we get back what we put out. But there is more. The key to successful manifestation is that we must have a clear intention and strong faith that it is done. It is not enough to merely put out loving and kind thoughts and expect specific outcomes in our lives.

If we put out love, we get love back, no doubt. It is also necessary to focus and blend our thoughts, feelings, intentions, and actions. And tailoring them to a specific outcome and giving thanks to our Father because we know it is so. After studying the works of the most prolific Science of Mind teachers of our time, it turns out there are four key factors to bring about a drastic change: feeling, thought, self-talk, and faith.

These combined dictate our state of consciousness, the timeline we are on, or the mansion we occupy in our Father's house. Human beings are wired to personalize just about everything, so it is no wonder that what shows up in our life turn into part of our identity and story. If we befall to sickness or injury, we have much to deal with, so much to overcome.

There is a doctor visit after doctor visit and the constant questioning of when and if we will get better. It is easy to fall into the trap of "this is who I am now" or "this is happening to me!" Conversely, many who are over-identified with health and fitness rarely, if ever, get sick at all.

Our identities, both good and bad, are the prisons that keep our real selves locked away – the infinite spiritual beings that we indeed are.

Every attachment that we hold to is a bar in the cell. The good news is that we can break free and begin to manifest the things we desire, what God desires for us, and what aligns with our souls, including perfect health.

OUR STORY AND REGULATING SELF-TALK

"Do not copy the customs and behaviors of the world but let God transform you as a new person by changing the way you think. Then you will know God's will for you, which is good and pleasing and perfect. "Psalms 46:10

Each of us has his or her own story. It is full of thoughts, feelings, and beliefs about us, the world, and our positions in it – accompanied by a narration of how things are, were and will be. We lay it out in a linear fashion, even though it is as much of an illusion as time itself. We have formulated something inside of our minds, and it does not exist anywhere else.

Even the most enlightened among us have some kind of tale that they relate to, regardless if they feed it any of their energy or not. This is a very human thing to do, even more, pronounced in American culture. We truly feel as if we are the central character of the story, thanks to Hollywood, television, and media – going back to our early literature and music.

The cliché example often used when describing how our beliefs and stories create reality is about money: the billionaire who lost it all, only to bounce back and amass more wealth than before because being rich is all that they knew. Their self-concept was and always had been that they were wealthy. They did not have to convince themselves of anything. It was what they expected as part of their story, and it was what they got.

Then there's the timeless tale of the lottery winner with the lack-consciousness that ended up bankrupt, addicted, and in jail, after only a couple of years because their concept of self was flawed. Their state of mind and quality of character was not aligned with God's wealth, so it was stripped away.

We see these examples of belief play out every day, but how about the story of a healthy person? What does their self-talk look like? This is one of the more challenging aspects of manifesting because it takes constant self-monitoring of our inner dialogue. We can start with this: when thoughts of sickness, worry, doubt, or pity arise (which they undoubtedly will), we do not react to them.

We simply acknowledge them, let them go, and silently affirm to ourselves what we wish to experience instead. We proclaim to God our natural state of health by using affirmations or affirmative prayer.

For example,

> ➢ *"What a blessing it is to be in good health, and I am forever grateful. Thank you, Father."*
> ➢ *"I know and trust that everything works for my greatest good. I relax and let go knowing I am in God's hands, and all is well."*
> ➢ *"My body serves me wonderfully, and I give thanks for its blessings."*

> ➢ *"Health and healing come naturally to me. It is my natural state, my God-given birthright."*

FEEL IT REAL

"And the prayer of faith will raise the sick, and the Lord will raise him up."
Romans 12:2

As mentioned previously, the feeling is a crucial ingredient of manifesting health. Some confuse mind metaphysics by thinking it is merely a matter of convincing ourselves that what we want is true.

But we are not lying to ourselves, nor playing a game of mental gymnastics. We create a healing effect by using thoughts, feelings, and intentions in harmony with our faith. It would be foolish to deny or ignore a current health threat because we believe that we are strengthening it by acknowledging it. We must go see the doctor and take the necessary medications, etc. But what we do not do is feed it our energy. It is the emotional charge, the reactivity to it, that keeps the karma alive and going.

It is possible to lie in a hospital bed and to feel as if you are at home, in good health, and enjoying time with your loved ones, while still knowing consciously where you are. It only takes a bit of courage to do. We have been taught by a material worldview that insists we are at the mercy of our environments, and so we react. From this mainstream perspective, we become victims and have forgotten about our spiritual essence.

We are like pinballs being bounced around by the myriad of external things that are seemingly out of our control, none-the-less our health.

But what if the opposite were true? What if it is our external worlds that react and rearrange themselves to our inner beliefs, that there is no separation between the two? Well, we can test it out for ourselves.

Many of us do not know how it would feel to be in an **"ideal state of health,"** as we have not allowed that to be part of our story for quite a while.  Or, maybe you are trying to feel yourself being healthy as you read this, only to be bombarded with thoughts of worry or how things "really are," without considering the higher perspective.

When we feel sick or in pain, it can be quite challenging to ignore and choose to feel something else. But what if, for just a minute, you can detach from everything and ask yourself,

- *"How would it feel if…"*
- *"Isn't it wonderful…"*
- *"Doesn't it feel great…"*

You can fill in the blanks…………………

"How would it feel to be healthy" is an excellent start, but this is personalized to you, and you can build off it however you would like. For instance, "Isn't it wonderful to be free of doctor supervision?" Or "how would it feel I could go about my day without having to worry about my health?" More specifically, "doesn't it feel great to board a flight to California, to see my nephew graduate from college and not have anything hold me back?"

The above relates to one of my clients, who we will call Stephen. Stephen was a man in his 50s who had moved out east away from his family on the west coast. Over the past year, he had been recovering from a shattered femur in which the therapy was pretty extensive. The feelings of guilt had overtaken him. He began to feel as if he was a burden to those he depended on and felt shame for not making it back to California to see his family.

After working with Stephen briefly, he confided in me that he felt determined to make it back home to see his nephew graduate from college.

Working with Stephen, we were able to disconnect from the feelings of guilt and shame and the physical discomfort that he felt from his injury. We began to feel Stephen healthy and free, even if he was not from a doctor's perspective.

In a couple of weeks, Stephen was able to turn his attitude around how he related to his injury, his spirits were boosted, and his progress had accelerated. He made it home to celebrate with his family without complication. The last I heard of Stephen, he had made a full recovery.

It is not about whether we think something is true. It is about becoming familiar with its feelings. The goal is to feel the emotions and the feelings alone while ignoring any type of storyline or thought pattern that may come with it. We are conditioning ourselves to feel a certain way that we might not allow ourselves to feel otherwise.

Silencing the inner chatter is vital to submerge ourselves in the feeling. An excellent way to do this is through meditation, in which a simple concentration of breath meditation will suffice.

VISUALIZATION

Visualization is used in all fields where some sort of progression or betterment of oneself is the objective. It is present in religion, personal development, and even professional sports. Tibetan Buddhists go into meditation to visualize  compassion. Tony Robbins (pictured) touts it as a key to his productivity and basketball player's replay, making the game-winning shot in their minds over and over. One could only conclude that there is something valuable to it.

The power of the mind is incredible! We have begun to scratch the surface of limits. Imagine scenes of ourselves being healthy and happy to physically moving energy within the body. The mind just maybe our greatest ally. It can heal us and make us sick, but it is up to us to use it.

To envision an illness dissipating from the body, imagine yourself as pure energy. Familiarize yourself with the parts of it that bring discomfort or pain. You can give these feelings any image that you think best suits them. You can picture the illness being removed outside of the body, dissolving and fading away. For broken bones and various injuries, we visualize the body reconstructing itself. We see the actual bone (or applicable body part) repairing itself. This is an intuitive process. However, it appears to you in your mind's eye is worth exploring.

Visualizing ourselves in healing light! This light can be coming from angels or other deities, or even God himself. Red,

yellow, orange, and green colors all have potent healing properties.

Lastly, we construct short scenes in our mind's eye of ourselves in good health. We might picture being surrounded by friends and family. Rejoice in our clean bill of health, or possibly a scene of us accomplishing something that our health has limited us from doing. Thus adding feelings of joy, relief, and freedom will all aid in this process.

Sound Healing

"And whenever the harmful spirit was upon Saul, David took the lyre and played it with his hand. So Saul was refreshed and was well, and the harmful spirit departed from him."
Samuel 16:23

Sound Healing is an ancient technique! It has already been proven to be an immensely powerful tool in western medicine with the massive boom of Music Therapy over the last century. The first Music Therapy program was founded at Michigan State University in 1944. Still, the practice of using music as a healing modality stretches back millennia.

Plato and Aristotle spoke of music as having a mathematical relationship with the Cosmos. They could relieve both mental as well as physical ailments. Shaman's of America and Africa's Indigenous cultures believed music had mystical powers 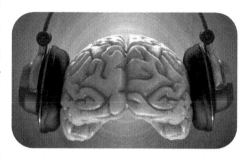 and often used singing and chanting with percussive instruments during healing ceremonies.

In the Bible, as quoted above, King Saul's ailments were healed by David's lyre. Christian hymns have utilized the healing properties of music, especially in a collaborative setting. The hymns' melodies, combined with the reality-altering power of the healing words themselves, created an extremely therapeutic effect on a congregation. While it is more evident in a group setting, hymns' healing power is present when they are recited after having been charged for millennia with this healing intention.

Though they didn't call it as such, this is a very similar practice to Vedic Mantra chanting in ancient India. Mantras are phrases or sounds, specific vibrations repeated to achieve a specific effect on the human energetic field. One such Mantra that has gained almost universal recognition is Om or Aum – the most important mantra. Sounds have originated from the beginning of time. Many modern philosophers have aligned with the opening of the Book of John: "In the beginning was the Word, and the Word was with God and the Word was God."

There is a massive amount of mantras, some meant for physical healing, some for spiritual healing, some for attracting love, some for attracting financial abundance. You can tailor which mantras you use depending on what kind of energy you are trying to manifest.

Alongside Mantras, you can utilize Singing Bowls. Singing Bowls have been recovered that are as old as five thousand years old. They range in shape, style, size, and, most importantly, tone. Each bowl is made to emit a specific frequency that helps an individual align with a specific healing frequency. You can see the effects of these frequencies in water. When a Singing Bowl is struck, it manipulates the water to move in precise, patterned movements.

Similar to these frequencies are lower frequencies that help regulate brain waves. From lowest to highest, those frequencies are Delta, Theta, Alpha, Beta, and Gamma.

These frequencies can be found on streaming services to aid in every aspect of life, from healing during sleep to enhancing dynamic performance during your waking hours.

FAITH

"Daughter, your faith has healed you. Go in peace and be freed from your suffering." Mark 5: 34

The most understated piece to manifesting is faith. Building upon and strengthening our faith trumps anything else we can do as far as mind spirituality is concerned. Without faith, it is unlikely that any technique will work anyway. People will typically try, and without seeing immediate results, they will proclaim that it does not work. Without faith, we do not have the patience and perseverance that it takes to bring about change. We must have the confidence that a Higher Mind, which we are one with, is working on our behalf and has always worked for us.

Faith is what allows us to relinquish control. To be clear, even though we are working to cause a healing effect within ourselves, we do not physically do any of it independently. We give it up to God to do for us. We are so accustomed to getting things done ourselves because who else will?

It is not until we see our way is not working or brought to our knees in defeat for many. They are only willing to let go and trust that something infinitely more significant than our ego is working it all out. Who we think we are and what we think we know at one time was beneficial; it served to protect us. Now, the older we get, the more these concepts seem to work against us- taking us out of the flow of life and closing us off to the Spirit of the Lord. It takes an incredible amount of faith to step out of all we have known, out of old clothes, and leap into the mystery.

To our favor, we have support in our corner. Those we came before who have left us with compasses and guide maps; descriptive layouts of the land, for what may seem like uncharted territory. Although faith works against all of our modern-day rationality, it is tried and true.
Building faith is a very personal matter for each individual. There are as many pathways to God as there are people. Likewise, there are numerous ways we can steady our minds to bring about healing.

For example, Christians focus and ground themselves in prayer or using a rosary to strengthen the mind. From a Hindu perspective, chanting and mantra connect us with higher consciousness. The Buddhist have been exploring and charting the mind in detail for thousands of years. The tools at our expense to aid in mind power are many; we only need to choose to pick them up.

CHAPTER 5
PSYCHOLOGICAL
BARRIERS TO HEALTH

PSYCHOLOGICAL BARRIERS

➤ Fear of losing
  independence
➤ Stigma associated
  with using some
  services
➤ Not wanting to be
  looked after by others
➤ Mental health
  problems

A number of psychological barriers can affect the physical, spiritual, and mental healing process of an individual. In my "day job" as a psychiatric nurse practitioner, I'm very aware that contemporary psychiatric interventions usually involve using pharmaceuticals to control mental health symptoms. However, they never assist in getting to the root of illness. However, many psychological symptoms will persist if the conditions they are attempting to alleviate are trauma-induced. The core of the issue is never addressed or resolved.

Research has confirmed that the use of spiritual healing as the sole treatment method effectively relieves short-term results of trauma, such as anxiety, PTSD, or depression. When used alone for people who have more pervasive and chronic diagnoses such as Schizophrenia, ADHD, or personality disorders, it can be helpful, but by no means a cure. However, when spiritual healing is used in conjunction with standard psychiatric care, it produces more significant and longer-lasting results.

Healing sessions can release repressed emotions that contribute to or are the underlying causes of long-standing mental health issues. Spiritual healing can add another dimension to these sessions. From my experience, it can be an effective method to expedite a person's ability to heal and have a higher overall quality of life.

Many, if not most, people experience traumatic events – both in childhood and adulthood – and are often unable to properly heal from these events on a mental or emotional level. Every individual reacts to trauma in different ways and has varied emotional reactions. However, no one can judge responses as right or wrong. They are simply what our minds and bodies do in their attempts to protect us from these isolated or repeated traumas. These trauma responses can be from simple stressful situations or more significant events that have created a psychological wound.

Anxiety or stress caused by trauma can frequently prevent people from relaxing enough to allow healing to manifest or for any kind of healing experience to be fruitful. When applied to a person suffering from stress or anxiety, spiritual healing can profoundly relax experience that helps people release these emotional trauma cycles. As said in Philippians 4:6-7, "Do not be anxious about anything…The peace of God, which surpasses all understanding, will guard your hearts and your minds." The atmosphere of safety, divine love, and acceptance provided by a spiritual practitioner help individuals remove trauma's adverse effects.

Stress is a significant factor. It has become clear that stress can significantly slow wound healing and be an underlying factor in almost every illness. Stress can cause several physiologic responses that create a negative impact on the entire body.

Do you know the signs of stress?

Agitation   Hopelessness   Self-neglect   Personality Change   Withdrawal

Some of the more serious physical manifestations of stress are a drop in insulin levels, which leads to higher blood sugar levels in your liver. The decrease can increase the risk of type 2 diabetes, increased heart rate, and blood pressure. It can also cause damaged arteries, leading to a heart attack, interfering with the reproductive system, or reduced sex drive.

Spiritual healing to reduce stress is a more effective method to deal with specific disease processes. It has a high degree of success when a trained healer performs or discovers how to use modalities and therapies.

Obviously, specific experiences have different impacts on one individual than another. Even the same event might impact individual differences in different life stages. What might have been an easy brush off the event at one point may trigger severely later on – or vice versa – making you feel helpless, defeated, or afraid. Smaller wounds can be solved quickly by getting time with a loved one or friend to heal. However, the larger ones may be too big to navigate and heal without professional help.

Psychological trauma disrupts the emotional body, which synthesizes our outer world and inner world experience and being in the moment of Now. It assists us in our balance and how we perceive our inherent self-worth. The Emotional Body is a bridge between our thoughts and our feelings about all things. When this is balanced, it will display empathy, emotional maturity, and openness with others.

When trauma throws off your emotional body's equilibrium, it can cause you to be anxious or to feel disconnected from other people. These traumatic wounds require someone to validate these events and your response to them.

Unfortunately, friends or family can (intentionally or unintentionally) invalidate your feelings and add insult to injury. Therefore, getting the help you need is best served by a professional healer – either mental, spiritual, or preferably, both.

Due to the stigma of seeking psychiatric or psychological help that our hyper-individualistic and materialistic society has created, many people find themselves seeking help. People tend to seek help at their general practitioner's office rather than therapists because physical issues are viewed as "more valid" than emotional, psychological, or spiritual ones. It should be clear by now, I hope that no one aspect of your physical wellbeing is less important than any other, and there is no shame in seeking help to heal yourself.

However, working through trauma can be painful, so many times, people try to avoid it. When an individual does not take the time needed to obtain help with trauma, the situation can worsen, and patterns that were once harmful become debilitating or life-altering. Avoiding help can result in the abuse of alcohol or drugs to feel better.

These situations can lead to personality changes and may progress to personality disorders. Many times we see the traits of these disorders before the individual is given an official diagnosis. Personality disorders can be defined as long-lasting, pervasive patterns of thinking, perceiving, or reacting. This can cause the person significant distress and impairing their ability to function daily.

Some people with severe trauma that leads to a personality disorder may not recognize a problem. Some can have symptoms or behaviors that fall under the umbrella of more than one personality disorder. Individuals diagnosed with these disorders have trouble relating to others, handling stress, poor self-image, and an inability to manage stressful situations.

However, medications are not always useful in even alleviating these symptoms, as they do not address the cause of the individual's state of mind. Instead, it just attempts to subdue them enough to not be a danger to themselves or others.

A 24-year-old woman named Lisa, with a Severe Depression and Anxiety diagnosis, came to me once seeking spiritual healing. She was already on a regiment of psychotherapy, anxiety-reducing medication, and SSRI's. Still, none of them seemed to be helping her get to the core of her problems. When she was young, she got into a severe car accident, which she, fortunately, survived with little more than a few scrapes and bruises.

Although she seemed okay after the fact, it wasn't the physical damage that lasted, but the emotional trauma. Ever since she's been unable to drive a car and has severe panic attacks at even the thought of driving. She refuses to sit in the front seat when being driven around. When provided the opportunity, she will take any other transportation method.

Childhood experiences often shape our adult years when it is tainted with trauma, neglect, or abuse. Some personality disorders can lessen or resolve with age. Some people will emotionally resist healing as a self-preservation method. It may also be a genetic predisposition towards a specific set of behaviors associated with a personality disorder.

If healing does not occur, these experiences and emotions are carried deep into our unconscious mind psychological crevices. Thus, affecting how a person thinks, perceives the world around them, and relates to others. Finding the source of our trauma and using a conscious awareness of how it manifests is essential.

Detrimental behavior patterns allow us to healthily express our thoughts and feelings to enrich ourselves emotionally, spiritually, and physically. There are several stages of working through trauma.

By understanding the process of working through trauma, it becomes easier to accept help to navigate these stages. It may be a complicated process, but this is where the power of spiritual healing comes into play, "for God gave us a spirit not of fear but of power and love and self-control." (Timothy 1:7)

Denial is at the forefront of the grieving process and is the beginning stage of awareness, and provides a defense mechanism. It is easier for the person to reject the problem such as divorce or death than to confront it. Before coming to me, Lisa refused to acknowledge that her aversion to driving was even a problem. She could take a bus, call a taxi service, or walk if she had to – even if her destination was miles away.

When a situation becomes impossible to ignore, it can become detrimental to both the individual and the people in their life. In Lisa's case, her family and friends began to get frustrated and resent her for being a burden of continually having to drive her around. Also, always having to deny invitations and miss out on aspects of life as her aversion to driving became more severe. This denial leads to the next stage of the process, as it becomes clear that something is wrong.

Anger is a common emotion when the issue at hand is acknowledged. When left untreated, anger or resentment can be built up and emotionally turned inward, as was Lisa's case. When Lisa realized that her avoidant behaviors were becoming detrimental to her life, she became angry.

First at the driver of the car that crashed into her so many years ago, then at her parents for not being able to avoid the oncoming vehicle, then at herself for not "getting over" her trauma. Passing through these various "substages" of anger allows us to recognize that there is no one at fault in some instances. Holding onto this anger is hurting no one other than us.

There is someone at fault in other instances, such as violent or abusive trauma, but it applies just the same. Holding anger at these individuals does nothing to them and only hurts ourselves. If this level of emotional pain occurs unchecked, it can manifest as various cancers and other systemic problems.

Relaxation techniques and spiritual healing can help alleviate this anger and allow us to experience and integrate ourselves or others' forgiveness. Understanding the truth of the situations or synchronicity of events in our lives is essential that spiritual healing and psychological treatment in conjunction can guide us toward. It requires a good deal of patience from a spiritual healer to successfully guide an individual out of this anger, as it is an exceptionally easily accessed and powerful emotion. Still, once there, the change is successful and dramatic. But it is not the final stage of the healing process, by any means.

Bargaining is the third stage of the healing process. An individual hopes they can avoid pain the trauma is causing without making any drastic changes to the comfort they've found in their patterns. In the case of issues relating to death, negotiating *will* change their behavioral patterns in exchange for a longer life or have their loved ones returned. This attempts to regain a sense of control that we feel we've lost (or maybe never had at all) after the traumatic incident occurred. During this stage, bursts of anger can come through as they find that their attempts to bargain do not change the reality of their situation.

It was much less intense in Lisa's case as hers wasn't a life or death situation, fortunately. She simply had immense difficulty attempting to find every possible way to project the sense that she had overcome her fear of cars and driving. However, continually found excuses for why she didn't actually need to overcome this issue.

It became clear that the more she tried to avoid confronting this issue head-on, the worse her situation would become. After reeling from the intensity of anger, sometimes it can feel as if the force propelling us has vanished, leaving emptiness inside.

Depression involves the feeling of sadness and being alone. People not understanding what the problem really is then rejected by others. Unfortunately, if left unchecked, these feelings of hopelessness may expand into suicidal thoughts or actions.

Fortunately, Lisa's combined regiment of psychotherapy and medication made this stage a little less severe. As she began releasing these old wounds, they resurfaced strongly. Having the support of the people in her life and God's Divine Love, she could not fall back into patterns of debilitating depression.

Throughout this entire process, I highly recommend using **therapy** in conjunction with spiritual healing, helping us develop coping mechanisms to handle stressors healthily. During therapy, we can gain insight and knowledge about what is contributing to our symptoms. We can discuss feelings and behaviors in a safe, non-judgmental environment.

By learning to cope with our symptoms, we can reduce behaviors, causing their functioning and relationship problems. Various psychological modalities are short term or long term, and both can be useful depending on their needs.

These include EMDR, EFT, Cognitive Behavioral Therapy, or Somatic Experiencing to heal and resolve your feelings. **EMDR** is Eye Movement Desensitization and Reprocessing. This can incorporate varied cognitive behavioral therapy elements with eye movements or other forms of rhythmic, left, right stimulation to unblock traumatic memories. **EFT** is the Emotional Freedom Technique, which is also referred to as tapping or psychological acupressure.

Like acupuncture, EFT focuses on physically stimulating meridian points, or energy hot spots, to create a balance within an individual's energy system. To practice this on your own, tap these points in this order: Top of the head, the eyebrows, the temples, the cheekbones, under the nose, the chin, the clavicle, under the arm, then back to the top of the head.

Cognitive Behavioral Therapy (CBT) helps process and evaluates your thoughts and feelings about trauma and is a common type of "talk therapy." It enables the person to become aware of negative thinking to view challenging situations more clearly, allowing them to

respond effectively. It can be a beneficial tool, either alone or in combination with other therapies.

Somatic Experiencing is a technique that focuses on bodily sensations rather than thoughts and memories about the event. The focus is on the concentration and feelings in your body so you can release the energy associated with the trauma by having an actual physical sensation.

Acceptance is the final stage of the healing process after trauma. After identifying the source of these feelings and patterns, she kept finding herself.

Lisa utilized spiritual healing to complement the medication and CBT she was undergoing. Spiritual healing helped her break her cycles of suffering and release the sadness and anxiety of her past. Positive affirmations, prayers, or mantras helped her realize that she was the key to the joy and love in her life, no one else – just as we all are. The warmth of the divine energy that began flowing through her during these healing sessions gave her an intrinsic feeling of unconditional love from the universal source.

Now, with this sense of spiritual support, Lisa's emotional pain has reduced significantly. Though the spiritual healing released a blockage and catalyzed her progress, she continues to see her medical provider. Her counselor helped her work through her feelings of emptiness, dealing with her parents' memories. Using psychological therapy and spiritual healing in tandem, we can transmute the seemingly negative situations in our lives into opportunities for healing and growth.

CHAPTER 6
PHYSICAL AND SPIRITUAL BALANCE

As we've already discussed, every aspect of your being influences all the others. The spiritual can influence the emotional, which affects the mental, controlling the physical and every possible combination. This is why it's essential as you work towards healing yourself to focus on your physical balance alongside the emotional and mental.

One such way to embody this balance is the ancient practice of yoga. Yoga is defined as a spiritual practice of union between the body and mind, which leads directly to union with God. However, there is no single way to practice yoga, and its origins come from anything but a single culture. It is a practice resulting from blending and borrowing from Buddhist, Jain, and Sufi traditions.

All forms of yoga have in common that they combine physical action with breathing practices and meditation. The goal of yoga is not to be physically fit like with a gym routine or exercise program. Instead to cultivate a spiritual awareness of oneself while expanding one's spiritual energy and focus.

Depending on your preferences and ability, several different yoga practices can help align your mind, body, and spirit to allow for a more comfortable healing process. You might also find, especially if you are a practicing Christian, that many of these yogic practices align very well with how you already live your life.

There are eight limbs or paths of yoga. They are Yama (abstinences), Niyama (observances), Asana (yoga postures), Pranayama (breath control), Pratyahara (withdrawal of the senses), Dharana (concentration), Dhyana (meditation), and Samadhi (absorption).

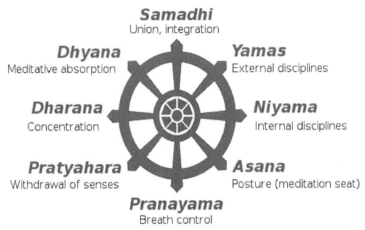

These branches can often be mixed as each individual finds what most benefits them and their healing process.

Yamas

Yamas are ethical rules and can be thought of as moral imperatives, basically the "don'ts." There are five Yamas listed in *Yoga Sutra:*

1. Ahimsa: Non-violence and non-harming other living beings.
2. Satra: Truthfulness and non-falsehood.
3. Asteya: Do not steal.
4. Brahmacharya: Chastity, marital fidelity, and sexual restraint.
5. Aparigraha: Non-possessiveness.

Niyamas

The second component of the yoga path includes virtuous habits and observances, basically the "dos," which are listed as:

1. Shaucha: Purity and clearness of mind, speech, and body.
2. Santosha: Contentment, acceptance of others, and acceptance of one's circumstances.
3. Tapas: Persistence, perseverance, austerity, asceticism, and self-discipline.
4. Svadhyaya" Study of self, self-reflection, and introspection of self's thoughts, speech, and actions.
5. Ishvarapranidhana: Contemplation of God/Supreme Being, true Self, and unchanging reality.

Each of the Niyamas help in personal growth.

Asana

Asana is a posture that one can hold for some time, staying relaxed, steady, comfortable, and motionless. Any posture that causes pain or restlessness is not a yogic posture. The correct posture for sitting meditation is to keep the chest, neck, and head erect into a proper spinal posture.

Pranayama

After the desired posture, the control of the breath has been achieved, basically, the practice of consciously regulating the breath. This is done by inhalation, then a full pause, exhalation, and an empty pause. This is done in several ways, such as by inhaling and then suspending exhalation for a period, exhaling and then suspending inhalation for a period, by slowing the inhalation and exhalation, or by consciously changing the timing and length of the breath (deep, short breathing).

Pratyahara

It is a process of retracting the sensory experience from external objects. It is a step of self-extraction and abstraction. Pratyahara is not consciously closing one's eyes to the sensory world; it is consciously closing one's mind processes to the sensory world. It empowers one to stop being controlled by the external world.

Dharana

As the sixth limb of yoga, Dharana is holding one's mind onto a particular inner state, subject, or topic of one's mind. The mind is fixed on a mantra, or one's breath/navel/tip of tongue/any place, or an object one wants to observe, or a concept/idea in one's mind.

Dhyana

It is contemplating, reflecting on whatever *Dharana* has focused on. If one focused on a personal deity in the sixth limb of yoga, Dhyana is its contemplation. If the concentration was on one object, Dhyana is non-judgmental, non-presumptuous observation of that object. Suppose the focus was on a concept/idea. In that case, Dhyana is contemplating that concept/idea in all its aspects, forms, and consequences. Dhyana is uninterrupted train of thought, current of cognition, the flow of awareness.

Samadhi

It is oneness with the subject of meditation. There is no distinction, during the eighth limb of yoga, between the acts of meditation, meditation, and the subject of meditation. Samadhi is that spiritual state when one's mind is so absorbed in whatever it is contemplating that the mind loses its own identity. The thinker, the thought process, and the thought fuse with the subject of thought.

ADDITIONAL YOGA INFORMATION

Hatha (meaning *force* in Sanskrit) yoga is a type of yoga that probably comes to mind when you think of yoga when people move through different poses (or asana). They focus on their breathing.

Hatha focuses on priming the body and mind and using the body as the primary vehicle for transformation.

Raja (meaning *king*) is a practice of yoga that centers on meditation and self-discipline. This form of yoga requires that a practitioner develop a strong sense of will that they cultivate through a set of ethics, virtues, and meditation. This set of virtues and practices as one stills the mind is very similar to the Christian tradition of praying, where one speaks to God. But when one practices meditation and stills all the external thoughts and influences, that's when God talks back.

Karma (meaning *action*) yoga centers on an individual's service towards others. As we've discussed previously, the idea of Karma is that one's actions have a direct influence on their wellbeing. The central concept of Karma yoga is that to better oneself, one lives one life as selflessly as possible, in service of others. Catholicism has an extreme focus on service to the poor as their path to God. As we'll discuss more later, helping others is really no different than helping oneself.

Bhakti (meaning *devotion* or *love*) is the practice of yoga that centers around connecting the bhakta (or practitioner) with the Divine. It is considered the least demanding of the yogic paths. The only requirement of the practitioner of Bhakti is to have an open, loving heart towards God – much like Christian practices of love and devotion to Christ and Mary. This is where Loving-Kindness meditation practices, the Serenity Prayer, and the Ho'oponopono can be utilized.

A more rigorous or intellectually minded individual might be more drawn toward **Jnana** (meaning *knowledge*, related to the Greek word *gnosis*) yoga.

Jnana yoga is a path towards spiritual harmony through the study of scripture and curiosity. People who ask big universal questions or often find themselves in Bible study groups discussing the Gospel's intricacies might find themselves already on this path.

Tantra (meaning *expand* or *to weave*) or Tantric yoga. Though you might first think of sexuality when you hear the word Tantra, that is only one tiny aspect of Tantra and far from the main focus. Tantra is the most encompassing branch of yoga. It incorporates the dynamics of many mystical practices with meditation, ritual, and breathing. It utilizes the relationships of energies both within an individual and outside of the individual.

However, all branches of yoga establish chakras or energy centers throughout the body. These are connected by points called

Nadis, which correlate with our modern scientific understanding of the nervous and circulatory systems, as we discussed in Chapter 1. Hatha yoga focuses on freeing this energy through physical movement. The breathing practices of Hatha and Tantra yoga use intention to open the chakras and allow these energies to move more freely throughout the Nadis.

This energy flows between **Ida** Nadi on the left side of the body and Pingala on its right side. The Ida (meaning *comfort*) Nadi is associated with feminine or moonlike energy. She can be stimulated by breathing through the left nostril. The **Pingala** (meaning *orange*) energy is associated with a masculine or sun-like energy. It can be stimulated by breathing through the right nostril.

These two energy flows indicate a balance when flowing correctly. They produce an equilibrium of energy; stimulate the Shushumna, or the body's central energy channel –connecting all seven chakras, which we'll discuss in detail in the next chapter.

When energy flows freely through the Shushumna, it releases the latent Kundalini energy, which leads to a state of blissful unity between a human and the divine. This experience is also referred to as Shakti and Shiva (the divine union of consciousness and energy). It is identical to the experience of charismatic Christians when entering altered states.

They speak in tongues, shake, and performing miraculous acts of healing. These sects talk about the experience of the Holy Spirit coursing through them. When these energies aren't able to flow freely and instead are stagnant or blocked, problems (mental, emotional, and physical) begin to arise, as discussed in earlier chapters.

CHAPTER 7
HUMAN ENERGY CENTERS

To, begin discussing the fundamentals of life, we need to first understand a few fundamental biological facts. All living and non-living objects in the Universe are made of energy. We learned this from Einstein's famous equation e=mc², or energy equals mass times the speed of light squared, which laid the groundwork for modern-day

String Theory. The matter is a form of energy-reduced to a slow enough vibration to become what we refer to as physical. Still, everything that acts upon that matter is also energy. This includes all physical and psychological processes such as thoughts, emotions, beliefs, and attitudes.

When we apply this to the human body, we realize every atom, molecule, cell, tissue, and body system comprises energy. When these energies interact with one another within our single, corporeal entity, they create what is known as the human energetic field or known colloquially as an aura. We are literally a walking talking energy field! Various cultures have various names in India for human energy, such as Prana or Shakti. In China, it is called Chi or Qi.

Newton's first law states that energy cannot be created or destroyed. All energy (including our own) is in a constant state of giving and taking as these exchanges and transmutations occur. The illusion of separation that we perceive from focusing solely on the matter and not energy completely ignores that metaphysical exchange. Each of our unique and ever-shifting energetic fields connects us all together as they interact with one another.

This fundamental truth is essential to your understanding as we begin our journey of spiritual wholeness and healing. It develops on a non-physical plane of your being and continues to deepen and grow. As we continue, we will begin to change and grow in our spiritual awareness -becoming more intuitive and possibly experiencing the unfolding of other spiritual gifts.

We have already discussed our various aspects of self and the needs of our being to include the physical, psychological, emotional, and spiritual body. However, we need to discuss a subtler aspect of our energetic field: the *etheric body*, which as we discussed in chapter 1, serves as the energy system for the physical body. It is here where, in many instances, the disease is first activated before it manifests noticeably at the physical level.

During an individual's emotional or mental healing, several things can be cleansed physically or etherically. Essentially, this refers to the first or lowest layer in the human energy field or aura. It is said to be in immediate contact with the physical body, sustain it, and connect it with higher bodies. This is why healing yourself emotionally with a professional is essential to your progress.

If stored as negativity in this etheric field, emotional pain can become severe and begin affecting the person's physical body.

Our energy is filtered by our emotional self and can block our healing mechanisms, both physically and mentally. How well we learn to accept, release, and transform harmful emotions. Emotions such as fear, hate, grief, or anger – into loving and compassionate energy are essential to accomplishing your life purpose.

Negative emotions can not only damage your health physically but will affect you spiritually. The mental body is your creative mind. As you grow, it can connect with the universal mind or the collective consciousness. It is here in the brain where we can create our own reality.

Our thoughts are so incredibly powerful. With this power, just as they can subconsciously cause us pain and suffering, they are equally capable of assisting us with the process of transforming that pain. Using the "I AM," which is our true self, affirmations, and creative self-visualizations, can help connect with the etheric body. An individual's ego has much less direct influence over this than in the other bodies, which is why it's so important to be aware of it and tap into this pure, untainted universal energy. This can be the location where miracles can happen as the spiritual self taps into the cosmic source of "all."

Another way to connect with your energetic field is by understanding and balancing the various energy centers called chakras, of which there are seven. These chakras or channels are the pathways to energy, which can get blocked for various reasons. The energy becomes stagnant and can cause significant emotional, physical, or spiritual problems. However, once recognized and understood, they can be cleared and improve the individual's physical health and vitality.

The first 3 chakras are the Root, Sacral, and Solar Plexus. They speak to your survival and will. The next 3 chakras are

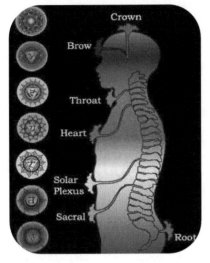

Heart, Throat, and Third Eye. They are considered higher centers, assisting with love, communication, and knowledge. The 7th chakra, the Crown, is the spiritual connecting point with mysteries beyond. The 1st chakra, the Root chakra, holds the basic needs of survival, safety, and security. It is associated with the color red.

It helps visualize each associated color when working with various chakras since each color has a different energetic frequency.

It is a phenomenon we were taught at a very young age the first time we learned about the rainbow. People who have blocks in their Root area struggle with financial instability, materializing goals, and may have a weak immune system. These individuals struggle with their core identity. Blockages that may be displayed manifest in the hip, back, knees, sciatica, or rectum. Phrases and affirmations associated with clearing the Root chakra are "I Am safe," "I Am Abundant," and "I Am supported by the Universe." And can be supported by Archangel Gabriel.

The 2nd chakra, or Sacral Chakra, deals with the energies of creativity, desire, intuition, and sexuality. It is associated with the color orange and physically covers the navel, lower abdomen, lower back, pelvis, kidney, bladder, lower intestines, and sex organs. Usually, this blockage manifests emotionally in issues of creativity or in relationship issues. Physically it manifests with female or male reproductive problems, spinal disc disease, or kidney problems. Affirmations used to clear the Sacral Chakra are "I Am Loved," "I Am creative," and "I Am joyful and passionate." And can be supported by Archangel Zadkiel.

The Solar Plexus is the 3rd chakra, located at the center of the belly at the lowest rib level, and is associated with the color yellow. It is the chakra of willpower, vitality, and personal power; and regulates your energetic field, digestion, and intuition (gut feelings). Organs are impacted by the stomach, liver, gall bladder, pancreas, and small intestines. Attributes in this area would be self-confidence, business sense, material, or financial ability. This is our spiritual power center, which you can draw upon to manifest goals. Blockages in this area stem from and result in fear of failing, lack of motivation, or inability to accept responsibility.

Physically, blockages could result in diabetes, indigestion, nausea, or obesity. Affirmations for the 3rd chakra are "I Am courageous," "I Am powerful," and "I Am ambitious." These prayers can be supported by archangel Uriel. The 4th Chakra is the Heart Chakra, at the heart space, which connects your body and mind with your spirit and is associated with the color green. It directs one's ability to love and accept oneself and others and can receive and give love. It is  the area that, when developed, can produce feelings of compassion for others.

Many healers can open up this chakra and feel compassion and universal love for others. Disease stemming from the heart chakra issues manifested as heart disease, lung problems, circulatory issues, shoulders, and upper back discomfort. Affirmations for working with the Heart Chakra are "I Am Love," "I Am open to giving and receiving love," and "I Am connected to all." And are supported by Archangel Chamuel.

The 5th Chakra is the Throat chakra, the center of people's ability to communicate and express themselves, and the ability to hear and receive from others. It is also associated with the color blue; it is also where the Sacral Chakra's creative energy can be manifested. Many people store anger and resentment in the Throat chakra and cannot verbalize and release these stored emotions.

Difficulty in this area would be an inability to speak up for oneself or express feelings or an inability to listen to others. Manifestations of illness would be in this area include sore throat, thyroid or parathyroid problems, jaw, teeth, and cervical spine.

Spiritual abilities that develop when this chakra is opened would be channeling or clairaudience (psychic hearing) from spiritual realms. Affirmations to aid in the development of this chakra are "I Am authentic," "I Am true to myself," and "I Am an open and honest communicator." These manifestations can be supported by Archangel Michael. The 6th chakra is located at the forehead above the eyes and is called the Third Eye. Associated with the color Indigo, the Third Eye is the place of insight and clairvoyance, seeing beyond physical realities and into other realms and understanding spiritual truths.

Energy blockages at this chakra include denial or truth, negative thinking, and the eyes, face, brain, immune system, and endocrine system. Physical illnesses resulting from a Third Eye blockage would include vision problems, hormonal imbalances, dementia, or brain diseases. It is the place of ecstasy and transcendence.

Clairvoyance or psychic gifts of knowing are all skills of this chakra. To aid in the development of these gifts, use affirmations such as "I Am connected to my higher self," "I Am a powerful co-creator with God and the Universe," and "I Am a spiritual being having a human experience." These affirmations can be assisted by Archangel Raphael.

The Crown chakra is the 7th Chakra, located at the top of the skull and is uniquely connected with multiple colors: Violet, White (the combination of all colors), or the full spectrum of the rainbow. It is believed that the soul comes into the body at the crown and then leaves at death by the Crown Chakra. It is the place where attitudes of giving or serving others and wisdom are found.

Blockages of this chakra stem from a fear of death or fear of one's intuitive abilities. Disease in this area manifests in the Central Nervous System and includes multiple sclerosis, spinal, and bone diseases.

Psychic abilities associated with a strong Crown Chakra include medium-ship and transcending the universe. Additionally, there are other energetic points of this chakra at the feet, palms, and soles. Healers may have enhanced or developed this chakra and can transmit energy. The Crown Chakra can be meditated on with affirmations such as "I Am Oneness," "I Am Whole and Complete," and "I Am connected to all that is." The Archangel Jophiel (pictured) can assist you with these prayers. You can learn more information about each chakra from Diane Stein's book, "Psychic Healing with Spirit Guides and Angels."

"An invisible thread connects those who are destined to meet regardless of time, place, or circumstance. The thread may stretch or tangle but will never break." Chinese proverb - *We are connected in the universe.*

CHAPTER 8
THE DARK NIGHT OF THE SOUL

As you embark on your spiritual journey of self-healing, whether through prayer, meditation, or other practices. It is almost inevitable that you will encounter what mystics have called The Dark Night of the Soul throughout the ages.

We have all experienced periods of depression, sadness, and grief throughout our lives. When it is brought on by adversity, trauma, or loss, it makes sense to us. Yet sometimes, this

"black cloud" seems to appear over our heads for seemingly no reason at all, or at least not a reason we can discern at the moment. When we understand the Dark Night of the Soul, we can realize that it never comes randomly or without purpose. The reason it comes is necessary for our spiritual development. Simply put: it is a part of life; it is our lesson here on Earth.

This spiritual phenomenon has been with humankind as long as we kept written records, and probably longer than that. When the Dark Night comes, we are asked to let go of aspects of ourselves that now no longer serve us. This grueling process must be done in our attempts to reach enlightenment or to become one with our Father. We are asked to step out of old clothes, be naked and vulnerable for a while, and put on something entirely new.

At one point, these aspects protected us, forming identities and patterns that allowed us to feel safe in conditions in which they were created. But now trap us in an old version of ourselves, old cycles that prevent us from moving forward out of fear.

Through this process, we become infinitely more significant than what we have been pretending to be. Of course, our job is never done until we can let go completely. Many of us have been undergoing this process for several lifetimes. When writing this book, I believe what we are going through with COVID-19, and other madness on Earth is our collective's Dark Night of the Soul. This chapter will explore how the Dark Night relates to all of us, our health, and our future.

THE SPIRITUAL PROCESS OF THE DARK NIGHT

"Dark Night of the Soul" is a term made famous by Spanish mystic St. John of the Cross Pictured), who wrote a poem by the same name in the 16th century. In his writing, St. John documented the process of seeking union with God and noted a period of despair  associated with inner-purification, external tribulations, and questioning the veracity of His existence. This is a term used almost off-handedly to describe life's ups and downs in the modern-day.

St. John made it clear, however, that *the* Dark Night is specifically about giving our lives to the Lord. I have no doubt about what we are going through collectively. You may be going through individually to lead us to higher consciousness and closer to God Himself. Spiritual seekers have been grappling with the Dark Night since the beginning of human history.

While teachers can explain the concept to us – and admittedly, it does help to know we are dealing with something very human and not alone. The pain is still genuine when we are in the thick of it, and no amount of prior knowledge or understanding can numb it. It is something we must trudge through, and trudge through alone at that.

It is a profoundly intimate experience. Although we cannot entirely rely on any human aid, we have God and the soul's luminous light to guide the way. The Dark Night of the Soul is a difficult phase, and it can feel as if our lives are falling apart. This is partially true because there are aspects of us falling away like leaves from an October tree. We must remember that these aspects are lower vibration and have been blocking us from the sunlight of the Spirit. The Dark Night is here to remind us that we know what is best; we have all of the answers inside us.

It is instinct to hold on to these perceptions and patterns, but this only makes the Dark Night sting more. Indeed, this is a blow to the ego, but we must let go and trust that a Higher Intelligence, the one within each of us, knows better than we do. The old leaves may fall away, but the tree knows once winter passes, new ones will come in the spring.

Without guidance or a strong intuition, it can be quite hard to comprehend just what the Dark Night is when we are going through it. Those more spiritually inclined will usually recognize it sooner than later. We can intuitively spot a Dark Night of the

Soul for many of us because it is not our first cycle and likely will not be the last.

HEALTH

A health crisis is ripe for a Dark Night of the Soul. We are in mourning. Maybe our health has limited us somehow, and we dearly miss the person we once were. The future seems bleak, and our minds cannot help but go over all of the things we could have done differently to prevent this, or all the things we would have done had we known this was coming. Nonetheless, there is an overwhelming feeling that things will never be the same. What is true is that after a Dark Night of the Soul, things cannot remain the same; *something* is coming to an end. But let us rejoice. What will end are only the things that must for us to evolve.

This is a natural cycle of life, death, and rebirth. It is not necessarily a physical death, but an egoic one. Although life is eternal, there is no separation anyway; they are simply two sides of the same coin. There cannot be heads without tails, there cannot be light without darkness, there cannot be beginnings without endings. During a Dark Night of the Soul, it may be challenging to know just what we need to let go of. It takes real introspection and investigation. As you know, being faced with a health issue forces us to reflect.

My sincere hope for you through this book is that you can answer the call. If our lifestyle has caused our sickness, a Dark Night lets us know we need to change and surrender to God what is not suitable. If it is your thoughts or emotions, the chapters of this book present practices and teachings that should make the letting go process easier. I must warn you, it is not a simple fix. It will not be solved in a single day.

This is a dedication to unlearning a fundamental aspect of how you perceived yourself, to work each day, little by little, toward who it is you were always meant to be. Have compassion for yourself during this process. Though Divine love flows through you, you are only human after all, and to be human is to make mistakes.

When you come out of the other side, you will feel amazing knowing that you are now in alignment with your Higher Self, in service to the Lord. It will make sense to you that what you had to encounter was imperative for your own individual progress and the collective evolution.

THE COLLECTIVE'S DARK NIGHT

Throughout history, families, communities, even nations have shared in Dark Nights of the soul, bonding most powerfully through tragedy and significant change. For the first time on this scale, being faced with the Covid-19 virus, we are experiencing a  Dark Night on an interconnected global level, causing many of us to become unhinged. We can only speculate about what is going on, and we must always question things and stay informed. But the truth is: none of us really know. What is possibly even more troublesome is that we have no clue we are headed.

We ask ourselves how much of this is in our control, and the answer is little. This makes us uncomfortable. Those of us on a spiritual journey go within. We trust God, take an assessment of ourselves, and contemplate what a more just and healthier world might look like. We are now being held accountable to be the change we want to see in the world.

It is interesting to see the spectrum of reactions to these events, as they mimic how we can choose to deal with a Dark Night of the Soul on an individual level.

We see denial, blame, anger, depression, addiction, etc., playing out on the world stage. We see people holding on to the old and fighting for dear life. We have to look at our faults, being forced to let go of what we once held as true and unquestionable. We have to make readjustments, having no clue what it is we are stepping into – this "new normal."

We are being forced to confront our collective karma and look It dead in the eye: racism, economic disparity, environmental challenges, how we treat our fellow man.

Our politicians and institutions' shady dealings are coming to light, as even they struggle to hold onto power. Everything is being uprooted and flipped over, and it appears the world has spiraled into chaos. For now, what has been hidden is coming to light.

People now have to sit with themselves and find time to heal, connect with, and align with their souls and true God-calling. Most importantly, our Mother Earth is given the space to heal herself. So, what can we do about our global Dark Night of the Soul? I speak to many of my clients about their Dark Nights, and I do not think there is any difference in how we approach the collective one; it is only essential that we do.

We are being pushed into a new level of consciousness, whether we like it or not. My hope for you is to develop a strong faith in God and yourself that is needed to endure this storm before we head into the new earth of "Christ Consciousness."

GRATITUDE, THE ANSWER TO WORRY

Even as true believers, those of us who know where we are going, are still faced with moments of doubt, frustration, anger, and worry. How could we not be? We are only human. We see things around us that we do not like, and it frightens us. It appears to be happening more and more, on a larger scale, and faster. Knowing that this is the Dark Night of the Soul for us as a species is somewhat comforting. However, we can still do things to bring more balance and grounding into our lives. So that we may weather the storm with dignity, compassion, joy, and a positive, helpful attitude.

When allowed to make choices and react to the chaos around us, take a moment to look inside yourself and really question whether the choice you are making is out of love or out of fear. If you find yourself paralyzed by fear and unable to find love anywhere, take a second to breathe. At this moment, gratitude may be our strongest line of defense. Developing gratitude not only allows us to mentally heal from the stress and negativity that is so prevalent, it sets up defenses against future physical illnesses. Gratitude is the cornerstone of developing a positive mental attitude, and as we have discussed in this book, our state of mind has a direct impact on our health.

You could say gratitude is the language of God. Blessings shower down upon us when we communicate with God that we are appreciative of all He does for us. If we are to believe that like attracts like, then by law, when we show that we are grateful we can only attract more things into our lives to be grateful for.

Feeling disconnected from our Father only leads to depression and hopelessness. When we fall ill, it is easy to feel further away from Him than ever before. Developing gratitude brings us back into the light, which heals us and allows for grace to happen.

This portion of the book is to serve as a reminder that we have good reason to at least be mindful of gratitude, not to guilt or shame anyone for letting it fall to the wayside, which is easy to do. It is a lot harder to practice this virtue. Still, there is also good reason we should be grateful.

We have numerous reasons to count our blessings, even if at times our blessings do not seem so plentiful. If we are being truthful with ourselves, all of us can at least find a few major things that we are grateful for, although the odds seem stacked against us. So why should anyone take on this practice? And a practice it is. Nobody develops an attitude of gratitude by osmosis. Daily prayer and journaling are excellent ways to develop this strength, and if we are disciplined about it, it happens rather quickly.

Knowing that the collective Dark Night is required for where we are going, we stay appreciative, hopeful, and willing to serve. This is an excellent time to reflect on who and what is in your life. Despite all else that may seem to be falling apart, gratitude is there to be a light guiding you through the darkness.

I would like for you to take a minute to consider whether or not you have been mindful of what you are grateful for. If you have not been practicing gratitude, then this is an open invitation to begin. It is never to late to develop gratitude.

The list below is something you can go briefly go over to get you started on your daily gratitude journey, or you may look over it regularly as a reminder.

- I am grateful for God's presence in my life.
- I am grateful to have woken up this morning.

- I am grateful for each breath that I take.
- I am grateful for the 2nd chance that the new day brings.
- I am grateful for the loving relationships in my life.
- I am grateful to have access to feed and clean drinking water.
- I am grateful to have a warm, dry place to sleep and a roof over my head.
- I am grateful for...

CHAPTER 9
THE KINGDOM OF HEAVEN IS AT HAND

What if I told you that there is a divine power within you right now? In John 14:12 of the King James Bible, Jesus says, "I say unto you, He that believeth on me, *the works that I do shall he also do; and greater works than these shall he do.*" This phrase is slightly different in each translation, but the core message is the same. If you believe in Him, and what better way to believe in this great teacher than to believe in His teachings, you will perform these same miraculous acts like Him.

You shall heal the sick, you shall make the blind see, and you shall embody God's love in physical form. Not only that, but you will do *more extraordinary* miracles than that if you simply understand that you are one with God, as is everyone and everything else around you. I know that the practices and beliefs I've spoken about in this book might be uncomfortable for many people.

Jesus is as real to me as any other Christian. He inspires me by infusing in me His teachings to do Spiritual healing. You can do this in the same manner by tapping into His essence, finding your connection with His spirit, and allowing Him in as your own personal inner healer. You can allow yourself to delve deeper into this higher aspect of your own divinity.

Some people might consider this to be heretical, especially more traditional Christians. But I want to clarify that everything I've spoken about in this book aligns with ancient teachings, including teachings Christ Himself said of. However, maybe not the interpretation of his teachings you've been taught.

Although divinely inspired by Christ to record and transmit his teachings to the best of their ability, the Bible writers were human. As history transpired, their inspired writings had to undergo the politically driven forces of the times. Could it be possible that their writings became altered in the process of writing the Holy Bible as we know it? I do consider this, although heretical, to be a possibility.

The original version of the text was written almost two millennia ago, and definitely not in English. In fact, English, or the language that eventually became English, didn't even exist then – and the languages that merged to become Old English haven't spoken anywhere near where Jesus lived. Jesus, or Yeshua, was born in Nazareth, where Aramaic was the common language. This means that the original version referred to as The New Testament was written in Aramaic more likely than not.

All of the subsequent translations have been done by fallible humans. As anyone who works in modern-day book translation will tell you, things are altered throughout each translation. Sometimes there simply are no words that accurately convey the meaning that exists in one language to another. Suppose we were to compare our modern version of The New Testament to the original version of the text. In that case, there's a very high likelihood that we might not even be able to identify them as the same book. Or if we could, we would see that many of Christ's original teachings have been removed, or at the very least obscured through metaphors and parables.

It is often intentional to match the individual's interpretation or to match some agenda they are attempting to pursue in their translation. This is the case with the First Council of Nicaea, who decided which books of the gospel should be canonical and which should not.

Among these books is the Book of Enoch, the Gospel of Judas, the Gospel of Mary, the Gospel of Thomas, the Dead Sea Scrolls, The Sophia (Wisdom) of Jesus, and others. Many of which are Gnostic teachings which were deemed heresy by the Council of Nicaea. Gnostics, a sect of early Christianity, find their name from the Greek word *gnosis* or knowledge. Though it is not a single standardized practice, just as Christianity today is not. Gnosticism is much more reflected in eastern ways of viewing the world – dealing not with concepts of sin and repentance like the main form of Christianity but in illusion and enlightenment ideas.

The original Aramaic speaking Christians, the Apostolic Church Fathers, and their teachings were disseminated by Paul and his converts to those who wrote in Greek or Latin. Many of them didn't understand Gnostic teachings. They seemingly changed the context of Christ's words in the New Testament that were not in the original Aramaic.

During the Council of Nicaea, our modern-day Bible's origins were organized. Many of these Gnostic texts were deemed not to be fit for the public Biblical canon. For what reasons they were not canonized, I'll leave that up to you to decide.

I say all of this not to convince you to throw away your Bibles and abandon your love for Christ. In fact, I want the exact opposite. I want you to look deeper into His teachings, look deeper into the actual lessons Christ taught and what that means for all of us today.

Each of the texts I mentioned earlier provides unique, universal insights into Jesus' teachings. Rather than the version of them that have 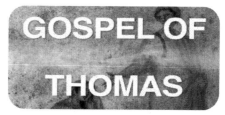 been passed down by this millennium spanning game of telephone. The Gospel of Thomas in particular.

It is a Gnostic text discovered in its entirety (along with over fifty other early, pre-Christian readers) in Egypt's ancient Nag Hammadi Library during the early 20th century. It is composed entirely of direct quotes from Christ himself, many of which align word for word with canon Gospels of the New Testament.

Readers of this text are told not to find salvation through their belief in Jesus as Messiah. But instead to find it *within themselves*, using metaphors and "hidden sayings" of the then *living* Jesus as a guide towards enlightenment, towards salvation. These original Aramaic texts taught a markedly "New Age" idea that Jesus was not uniquely gifted as the Son of God. It was that He was the first, the one meant to shepherd us into a New Age of peace and love.

Jesus taught that we are all Children of God, we all have a divine relationship with the Holy Spirit, that we are all one with it. Jesus was reflecting much older wisdom than even Himself. The state of consciousness He achieved is what we now call Christ Consciousness. It is a state just the same as that of Nirvana or other similar eastern enlightenment states or ascension taught in Buddhism, Hinduism, and several other eastern traditions.

The term Christ is a title bestowed, not a name that Jesus was born with. A Christian person can give and receive the universal love of God truly unconditionally. Love thy neighbor means just that. This love is a divine gift that we all hold within ourselves. An individual we call "Divine" embodies this unconditional love and compassion through their every action.

What Jesus attempted to convey to everyone, which might have gotten lost in translation or intentionally misconstrued, is that we are not merely our bodies. We are manifestations of the divine oneness of the universe, and we must allow that light to shine through each of us.

As we as individuals undergo this process of awakening, so too does the collective. The Bible speaks of Jesus' return, of a second coming that will mark the end of days, of which I do not disagree. I simply want to possibly readjust how we perceive the idea of that return. Is it possible that Christ's return is not a literal return of Jesus himself? Still, a return of the Consciousness he introduced into the world? Might the "end of days" they speak about not be literal destruction of the world, but of the systems and ways of thought that keep us stuck in these mindsets of lack, fear, and hate?

The meaning of the second coming maybe is marked by the astrological conjunction of Jupiter and Saturn that occurred on December 21st, 2020 when a new six-hundred-year cycle began. The conjunction of Jupiter and Saturn occurred in the astrological sign of Aquarius, something that had not happened

since the 15th century, just before the Renaissance began. This was the same conjunction that occurred above the birth of Christ.

There have been many mystical, astrological, and religious interpretations of the "second coming." Still, maybe it is as simple as this: individuals have been designed by the light and love of God. Jesus said, "there is a light within man, and with it, He lights up the world. If He does not shine, He is in darkness." In the Gospel of Thomas, Jesus says, "When you make two one, when you make inside as the outside, outside as inside, upper as the lower." And when you make the male and the female into a single one, so that the male is not male and the female not female, then shall you enter "the kingdom."

Now, as we rise out of the illusion of separation, He desires all individuals to recognize that we are, in fact, manifestations of this light and love. We must externalize and unfold our divine higher self through our body, manifesting His form in this physical form. This second coming of Christ is the return *in each of us* to this divine frequency of love, compassion, and understanding. We are all these divine beings; we are all Christ.

Upon discovering this presence within, we shall see this expression without all around us.

Christians or non-Christians who integrate and utilize these higher understandings of the Church Father's teachings to invoke peace on Earth will lovingly discover their connection to the Heaven within, which is the presence of God. Therefore, Hell is not a physical place of fire depicted in books but is the spiritual state of separation from God's love. We have free will to choose where we would like to reside.

This realization, this freedom from fear and union with love, is how you discover your ultimate purpose in life and ascend in a manner as the master Jesus. When an individual is willing to shed all of the illusions of division, we exist for one another because we are all one, which is the beginning of enlightenment. The next step, after awakening, is to develop your character as in the ways Jesus discussed that by doing good to others and the Earth as all the masters who came before us.

This is the primary essence of ascension or enlightenment. Then comes the act of finding your way to serve humanity with your ability, opportunity, or education. I have accomplished this by tapping into my gifts as an energetic healer and helping the collective by healing the individual. To find your purpose, the surest way to do so is by spending time in meditation and prayer, communing with God. Remembering who you indeed are and why you are here is essential to remember as you embark upon this self-actualization journey.

You are the sum total of so many lifetimes. Through each lifetime, you have been working towards finding the most accurate form of this expression to improve others' destinies. As you advance along the path and develop your relationship with the Master, it becomes less of a devotee/teacher relationship and becomes a partnership of oneness.

You must be patient with both yourself and God as this process occurs. It is not a singular moment of enlightenment from which you never go back. This place of conscious oneness is achieved over time and does not abide by our perception of time. We are still incarnated in human bodies, in this reality of constant upheaval and suffering. There will be days in which you can embody this love and compassion more quickly than others. Just as you strive to have understanding for those around you, you must have compassion for yourself.

It is a constant motion and practice as you attune to the love and light that Jesus embodied. As you develop your mind in His consciousness, your service is the Christ in action. And as you begin to incorporate this Christ Consciousness, you will notice magic occurring all around you. And I don't mean the magic of witches and wizards, of Merlin and Harry Potter, no I mean the real magic of God, the miracles of Christ. The miracles you read about marks him as the son of God were given to Christ because he served the collective and public ministry.

Jesus called in the Holy Spirit to assist and raise the consciousness and vibration to assist in this acceleration. When he said, "I am the way," he was not speaking about himself; he was speaking the name of God: I Am That I Am. This understanding that I Am the way, the embodiment of this loving life force, is the path towards Christ Consciousness.

Through your attunement to his divine whispers in your prayers and meditation, the Holy Spirit will assist you in your services, as happened with Christ and His disciples (pictured). You will be assisted by all of those of the highest, including those in the angelic realms. This is the cosmic moment, and it begins now! The stars and planets are contributing their light to the star to Bethlehem.

This is the ushering in of the new time for the earth, so tap into the love being sent forth to awaken each from your indifference. Become that power for yourself by stepping into your power for yourself and making a difference for humanity.

CHAPTER 10
INTEGRATIVE HEALING
FOR THE FUTURE

Here we are, those of us who decided to come to Earth and volunteer to be here during this unique point in history – amidst a global pandemic. We were here during wars, corruption and dramatic political turmoil and helped each other magnetize our fullest potential. It has not been an easy road to travel, there have been many tears and pain, but we're moving through it with courage, love, and compassion.

My hope is that each person who reads this book comes to the realization that *you*, yes you, are part of the change. In the depths of your pain and suffering, you would awaken to a message and call to action. You are being allowed to reach your highest potential. We are aligning with the divine plan at this cosmic moment in history. As our population increases and medical services are stretched to their limits, it will be critical for individuals to learn how to care for their bodies to reduce illness.

At this time, you may be curious as to just *how* you will discover your innate power to heal. As you finish this book, I hope that I have begun to remember what was unknown or forgotten. That you have recognized the body has its own divine intelligence and therefore knows all the answers to what it needs. Becoming aware of your divine spiritual connection will allow you and the Divine Source to work collaboratively together in harmony.

Spiritual awareness helps enrich our lives in a myriad of ways. This is why finding a spiritual affiliation that fosters your spiritual growth is so essential.

There are many traditional and non-traditional religious organizations, from temples to churches, 12-step support groups, meditation, and yoga centers. There are so many options to choose from, so as I've stated before, always follow the choice guided by love, not fear; otherwise, it is incredibly easy to be confused by misinformation.

Integrating your entire being for your optimal health, physically, emotionally, mentally, and spiritually, is the "Medicine of the Future." Although they will still have their place, surgery and medications will hopefully be a last resort in the future. Patterns on a cellular level that are causative of the disease will be the first line of treatment. As a collective, however, we will focus our attention not on treatment but on prevention. Balancing ourselves and educating other people in the importance of keeping their energy balanced and healthy will be a regular part of daily physical hygiene.

It will involve many complementary practices, as well as spiritual or energetic healing. In the years to come, I have no doubt that spiritual or energetic healing will emerge with a more prominent role in mainstream health care. Spiritual healing and conventional medicine must work together in harmony. And is the most direct path for each of us to attain our potential and transform ourselves, reflecting what heaven has in store for each of us.

If you choose to work with a spiritual healer, the healing power within you is reflected by the practitioner. The healing they enable within you is your true self at its fullest potential. All the healer does is remind you to do the healing work and assist you in Remembering the Kingdom of God. At this time, when you become truly open, you can tap into this expanded space and feel the immense power that lies there and allow amazing things to transpire.

Navigating the management of your symptoms and the emotional, physical, or spiritual patterns that enabled them will allow you to discover your own divine inner healer. The knowledge that has been provided to you within this book is only the beginning. Understanding your own energetic bodies' healing power and identifying what patterns you hold on to prevent you from healing is only the beginning. Finding a routine practice of prayer, meditation, or affirmation. Spending time getting in touch with your body, mind, and emotions through yoga and having faith in yourself and the Divine. All begins with a level of awareness and a willingness to leave behind what no longer serves you.

Passed down through the ages, we have been given life-transforming activities and practices that are simple enough to perform if we can put our egos aside to be consistent and disciplined in our journey. Though it may have been mistranslated and misconstrued along the way, these practices still hold immense power, as they allow us to connect with our own "Christ Consciousness." By putting aside our preconceived notions of what is true and right. We then open ourselves up to a healing force of unconditional love that has been waiting for us all along.

If you allowed yourself to know how much God wants you to accept this divine opportunity, you would receive His anointing as gratitude for healing yourself. Also, for healing the collective, and for your service to the "Light." Respond to your inner promptings to consciously decide to make it happen. All we must do is show up for ourselves and each other every day. Knowing that God's presence and strength can assist us with this letting go of our past fear-based decision making processes and rise above internal resistance to shine at the moment.

Every human can permanently heal their various imperfections or physical disharmonies when they realize they are self-inflicting these problems by separating from their divine nature.

We can blame this separation on allopathic medicine, saying that illness needs a cure without seeking the disease's underlying problem. We can say prevention has not been given priority from the onset. Still, it aims to entertain it only after many medical conditions have arisen. But there is no use in placing blame anymore. We must simply act upon what is and move forward.

To move forward, we must each take responsibility for doing our individual part. We can see how the physical, emotional, mental, and spiritual imbalances are not separate. They are interwoven and impact the functions of the entire body. We can utilize the energy sources throughout our body, the chakras, and use music and prayer to correct each imbalance. If we only listen to our body and our internal whispers from the divine, we can manifest our perfect health.

There will be conscious decisions and choices for each of us to make regarding diet, exercise routine, or spiritual practice that may be best in our life. And there is no right or wrong answer for each individual, simply what resonates with them and finds most beneficial. Our goals must not be based in a mind-frame of lack, but instead in that of abundance, utilizing positive affirmations and visualizing to manifest your ideal outcome or solution.

By your own awareness, you will determine the underlying issue of our suffering and go within to access your own solution. As you find balance in your four bodies, physical, emotional, mental, and spiritual. You will discover more peace in your life through all these methods discussed, discovering your connection to your spirit and Divine Source.

Heal your separation from your higher self and communicate with it by going within. This will allow you to tap into the sacred knowledge that lies there, that has always been there waiting for you to remember it.

Techniques to accomplish this plan for healing will begin to flow into your consciousness. Jesus said, *"It is not I but the Father within who does the work,"* and the power of the Father is within each of us. Though many did not believe that to be the case for millennia. Things are changing, however, as we begin this new journey, strengthening into what is marked by the dawn of the Age of Aquarius, or the Golden Age, with Saturn and Jupiter's conjunction on 12-21-20. You can take the leap and know you are needed for this next part of the Divine plan.

God has chosen each of us to accept this responsibility and plan our rebirth, of turning our lives around. Also, of turning all of humanity towards the path of love and compassion. We are the microcosm of the macrocosm, as above so below. As we transform our lives, we can assist others to do the same. Are you willing to do your part to fulfill in creating Heaven on Earth?

REFLECTIONS

U pon concluding the book, I would like to take some time to reflect with you on some of what you have learned about yourself and your unique spiritual journey towards healing. Likely, you have been doing a lot of reflecting and self-discovering along the way already. This will benefit you going forward as everything unravels and begins to be clearer to you.

I wish that you not only find health, happiness, and peace but that you have a solid grounding in who you are as a spiritual being and in your soul's purpose. Right now, you can start to ask yourself some of these questions and come back to them for when you need a check-up to gauge where you are at.

> ➢ **Are you discovering things about yourself to achieve fulfillment in your life?**
> ➢ **Are you seeking deeper meaning in life beyond just the physical?**
> ➢ **Are you expressing the things that are on your mind? Whether speaking, writing or other creative forms of expression?**
> ➢ **Are you considering a yoga practice or some form of daily gentle exercising such as walking?**
> ➢ **Are you changing the way you have been thinking and viewing things by focusing your thoughts more positively?**
> ➢ **Are you making time for gratitude in your day?**

- ➢ Are you growing in awareness of God's presence?
- ➢ Are you pursuing your divine purpose?
- ➢ Are you in a relationship with God that is the source of happiness in your life?
- ➢ Are you struggling with anger or resentment? If so, what spiritual tools can you use to help you?

And remember, this is an ongoing practice. You can come back to these questions whenever you feel the need to check-in with yourself.

MEDITATION

This exercise will assist you in balancing the four bodies – Physical, Mental, Emotional, and Spiritual – and in regenerating your wellbeing. God has assigned four of His Archangels to aid in balancing individuals to lead harmonious lives. In Zechariah 2:6; Daniel 7:2, and Matthew 24:31 God mentions the four winds of heaven, which align with these four archangels and the four cardinal directions.

Always begin with a prayer to set the intention of your meditation setting. Soft, instrumental music will assist you in deepening the experience.

To begin, sit comfortably in a chair, relaxing your entire body. Keep your arms and leg uncrossed in an open position and ready to receive. Keep your back erect and close your eyes.

Now relax.

Take long, slow, deep breathes that fill your entire being. As you breathe, allow your consciousness to expand and go deeper within to the depths of your being. Feel the love pouring forth from the heart of God.

As you breathe in, visualize bringing this love to each and every cell of your being. As you release and let go of anything that is weighing you down, or clouding your mind. Envision yourself surrounded by a pulsating white light which embraces you with a force field of protection.

Beginning in the East, Archangel Raphael represents the element of air. Raphael assists the clearing of the mental body, breaking free from unhealthy thoughts or habits that are blocking your progress in life. He inspires you and empowers you to accomplish your divine purpose

Moving to the South, Archangel Michael represents the element of fire. Cleansing each gland, organ and cell of the physical body. Michael encourages you to be courageous and take risks to be a stronger individual. The holy light of God blazes and corrects every imbalance.

Moving to the West, Archangel Gabriel represents the element of water and assists with the emotional body. He inspires you to be more receptive to God's message – both in your dreams and in the waking world. This is your communication with God as He supports you in balancing negative emotions, and the worldly drama that no longer serves you.

Moving to the North, Archangel Uriel represents the Earth. He clears your spiritual body of all the memories of the past, helping you with His divine wisdom of solid truth. Uriel brings stability into situations of your life so you can prosper.

As you now balance these four elements of your body, bringing them into physical, spiritual, mental, and emotional balance. Intend for them to be healed, transformed into perfection of your I Am presence.

Gently return your consciousness back to your body and the room. Feel yourself lighter and harmonized. Experience the harmony of your divine self.

ROUTINE

Part of discovering your power to heal comes through a daily routine of spiritual practice, of which there are many. No one activity or technique is more superior to any other. A spiritual way can be as simple as taking a walk or smiling at yourself in the mirror. The only important thing is that you develop a realistic routine for yourself and one you feel you can stick to.

For example, upon awakening, we set an intention for our day. What would we like to experience, and what kind of energies do we want to carry with us throughout the day? Compassion, forgiveness, acceptance, optimism?

After setting our intention, we go into prayer to commune with our Father. We surrender our will and lives to Him. We ask him that we be of service and to be a vehicle for his divine love. We ask for protection and guidance. We can do this with meditation or separately. If we eat in the morning, we look for something healthy and nourishing. We bless our food, give thanks for it, and be mindful as we eat.

In the bathroom, while getting ready for the day, is a great time to practice affirmations? The best time to do them is in the morning after clearing our heads and before we are bogged down by the day.

Afterward, we may go for a walk or practice yoga or any activity that helps connect our body and mind. Throughout the day, we are mindful of our thoughts and feelings. We make sure to pause, connect with the breath, and remain present with our experience.

At night before retiring, we should check-in with ourselves. We can do this with prayer, journaling, meditation, or visualization. This will help us to sleep well. Practicing good sleep hygiene is a necessary form of self-care.

Some days we may feel that it is important to be alone. But we still do our best to connect with others. We must spend time with our friends, family, loved ones, spiritual community, or support system. Being able to talk openly about our feelings is the key to spiritual health.

I left the rest of these pages blank intentionally, to give you a space to begin heal. Write down anything you want: a routine you might want to establish, any thoughts you might have on what you've read in this book, things in your life you might be grateful for.

MY REFLECTIONS

MY REFLECTIONS

MY REFLECTIONS

MY REFLECTIONS

MY REFLECTIONS